ABOUT THE AUTHORS

Leonie Warren M.Ed. is a Research Officer in the Equality Studies Research Centre, University College, Dublin. Her current work is in the area of gender and mathematics, having previously worked as a teacher of mathematics at second level. She has been involved in the design and facilitation of an in-service training programme for women interested in educational management and has published in the area of women's careers in teaching. She co-ordinated the Irish contribution to the Balance Project, which developed classroom materials on gender equality for second level schools and was joint editor of the publication *Balance: Who Cares?*

Eileen O'Connor M.Sc. in Ed.Mgt., is Deputy Principal of Greendale Community School, Dublin. Her areas of interest include education, teacher training and women in management. She has been involved in the design and facilitation of inservice training programmes for teachers in the areas of school administration and student welfare, most recently with ISIS: *Integrating Students Into Schools*, a Comenius training programme for second level teachers. She has also designed and facilitated an inservice training programme for women interested in educational management.

STEPPING OUT OF THE SHADOWS

Women in Educational Management in Ireland

Leonie Warren
Eileen O'Connor

Oak Tree Press
Dublin

Oak Tree Press
Merrion Building
Lower Merrion Street
Dublin 2, Ireland
www.oaktreepress.com

© 1999 Leonie Warren and Eileen O'Connor

A catalogue record of this book is
available from the British Library.

ISBN 1 86076 152 6

All rights reserved. No part of this publication may be reproduced or transmitted in any form or by any means, including photocopying and recording, without written permission of the publisher. Such written permission must also be obtained before any part of this publication is stored in a retrieval system of any nature. Requests for permission should be directed to Oak Tree Press, Merrion Building, Lower Merrion Street, Dublin 2, Ireland.

The publisher and authors gratefully acknowledge the
support of the Department of Education and Science
in the preparation of this publication.

Printed in the Republic of Ireland
by Colour Books Ltd.

Contents

Acknowledgements .... *xi*
Preface... *xiii*
List of Tables and Figures .... *xvii*

Chapter 1: Introduction 1
   Outline of Further Chapters 3

Chapter 2: The Context 5
   Introduction 5
   Research in Educational Management: Theoretical
      Approaches.. 6
      The Non-feminist Approach...................................... 7
      Liberal Feminism and Research............................... 7
      Radical Feminism and Research............................... 8
   Women's Career Development.. 11
   The European Dimension 14
   Inequality in Educational Management: Contributing
      Factors... 17
      Responsibilities and Mobility 17
      Socialisation and Women's Careers 18
      The Conceptualisation of Management................... 21
   Summary... 23

**Chapter 3: The Teaching Career: Findings and
Analysis**... 25
   Introduction 25
   The Feminisation of the Teaching Profession............... 26
      The Overall Pattern of Feminisation...................... 26
      The Feminisation Process: The Primary Sector..... 28
      The Feminisation Process: The Secondary Sector .. 29

    The Feminisation Process: The Community &
       Comprehensive Sector 30
    The Feminisation Process: The Vocational Sector 31
    The Rate of Feminisation 31
Career Continuity and Discontinuity 33
Profiles of the Teaching Body: Primary and Secondary
    Sectors 34
    Profile of the Teaching Body: The Primary Sector 34
    Profile of the Teaching Body: The Secondary Sector 37
Career Continuity and Discontinuity in Community &
    Comprehensive and Vocational Sectors 40
    Method of Presentation of Data 40
    Career Continuity and Discontinuity in the
       Community & Comprehensive Sector .... : 41
    Career Continuity and Discontinuity in the
       Vocational Sector 44
Summary 48
    Feminisation 48
    Longitudinal Data: Primary and Secondary
       Sectors 49
    Loss of Career Time: Community & Comprehensive
       and Vocational Sectors 50

**Chapter 4: Women and Promotion: The Role of
Women Teachers in Schools 51**
Introduction 51
Anomalies in the Promotion System 51
    The Primary and Secondary Sectors 52
    Community & Comprehensive and Vocational
       Sectors 53
The Current Situation 53
Factors Affecting Recent Changes 58
    The Process of Rationalisation and Amalgamations 58
    Types of Principalship and Gender in the Primary
       Sector 59
    Age and Promotion: A Complex Relationship 61
    Age and Promotion: The Primary Sector 61
    Age and Promotion: The Secondary Sector 64

Age and Promotion: The Community & Comprehensive Sector 65
Age and Promotion: The Vocational Sector 68
Applications and Appointments to Promotional Positions 70
Applications and Appointments: The Primary Sector 70
Applications and Appointments: The Community & Comprehensive Sector 71
Applications and Appointments: The Vocational Sector 73
Summary 76
Summary: The Primary Sector 76
Summary: The Secondary Sector 77
Summary: The Community & Comprehensive Sector 78
Summary: The Vocational Sector 79

Chapter 5: Women in Educational Management: Perceptions and Barriers 81
Introduction 81
Sources 82
Structural Barriers to Women in Management 82
The First Filter: The Application 83
The Second Filter: Shortlisting 84
The Third Filter: The Interview 84
The Fourth Filter: The Appointment 85
Summary: The Four Filters 86
Effects of the Irish Educational System 86
Attitudes of Women to Applications for Principalship 87
Religious Sisters as Role Models 88
Women's Perception of Management 89
Women's Attitude to Career 90
Perceptions of the Position of Principal and Lack of Support 91
Style of Management and its Impact 92
Power Relations in Education 92
Perceived Attitudes of the Gatekeepers 93
Power Relations among Colleagues 94
Summary 96

Chapter 6: Women into Educational Management: Positive Interventions 99
Introduction 99
A Pilot Leadership Training Programme for Women 101
Objectives of the Programme 102
Programme Philosophy and Methodology 103
Programme Content and Presentation 105
Programme Evaluation 106
Summary 110

Chapter 7: Conclusions and Recommendations 111
Introduction 111
Conclusions 112
   The Feminisation Process 112
   Women's and Men's Careers 112
   Gender and Promotion to Principalship 113
   Other Promotional Posts 114
   Applications for Promotion 114
   Women's Attitudes and Choices 116
   A Positive Intervention 117
Recommendations 118
   Collection of Data and Research 118
   Planning for Equality 118
   Resources for Support Structures for Principals 119

Appendix 1: Collection of Data 121
Appendix 2: Data for Tables 3.7a, 3.7b, 3.8a and 3.8b 123
Appendix 3: Qualitative Methods 124
Appendix 4: Women into Educational Management:
  Programme 125
Appendix 5: Evaluation Form 126
Appendix 6: Evaluation Form 2 128

Bibliography 131

To

Bridget and Margaret

for their vision and independence of spirit

ACKNOWLEDGEMENTS

The research and training programme on which this book is based was commissioned by the Equality Committee of the Department of Education and Science. We thank the members of that committee, in particular the Chairperson, Denis Healy, for their support. Two committee members who worked closely with us, Maureen Bohan and Hilda McHugh, gave generously of their time and expertise.

The assistance we received in working on this project was immense. It was given generously and cheerfully, particularly at times when the pressure of other work made our requests almost impossible to grant. To those who helped and supported us, we express our sincere thanks. David Tuohy, Education Department, University College Dublin, made an important contribution to the shaping of the project in its initial phase and we acknowledge his influence in this. Anne Gold, Institute of Management, University of London, played a key role in the development of the training programme for women outlined in Chapter 6. The gathering of primary data was an onerous task for the Chief Executive Officers and staffs of Vocational Education Committees, the principals and staffs of community and comprehensive schools, and for the public servants in the Department of Education and Science. We appreciate their unfailing courtesy and co-operation in assisting us.

Maura Mulcahy and Moira Leydon of the Association of Secondary Teachers of Ireland and Deirbhile Nic Craith of the Irish National Teachers' Organisation responded generously to our requests for information. Others who supported us in different ways include Teresa McCormack of CORI, Brian McNamara of Holy

Child Community School and Anton Carroll of Greendale Community School.

A number of friends and colleagues assisted in the difficult task of reading and commenting on drafts. They include: Úna Collins, Pat Diggins, Margaret Healy, Margaret Hogan, Maureen Lyons, Aidan O'Connor, Bernie Quinn, Bride Rosney and Ann Warren. We thank them for their helpful insights which were of great assistance to us in completing the work.

To the teachers and managers who shared their thoughts with us, your commitment and sincerity were inspiring. Thank you.

We could not have managed without the constant encouragement and support of our families: to Áine, Willie, Aidan, Dermot and Deirdre, a sincere thank you.

PREFACE

John Coolahan

This is a welcome and timely study of the occupational status of women in the education system at first and second level in Ireland. A number of research studies in recent years have established the fact that while women are increasingly forming the great majority of staff within the teaching force, the proportion holding leadership positions is actually decreasing, from an already small base. This is an issue of importance not just for the personnel involved but for the overall well-being of the system. The schooling system, which has such a formative influence on young people, should not exemplify sex stereotypical processes and, at a time when high quality leadership is crucial in schools, the whole pool of talent should be available and drawn upon to fill leadership positions.

The objectives of this research are well targeted. They involve: a comparative analysis with the experience of other European countries; an exploration of possible reasons for gender imbalance; the establishment of the detailed factual position; an exploration of women's attitudes in relation to leadership; and the promotion of informed public discussion on possible strategic interventions to redress the imbalance. I believe that the study realises these objectives very successfully. The book is well researched, comprehensive in treatment, incisive in its analysis and well-rounded in its recommendations. It has the further virtue of being very readable. At a time when the schooling system is becoming more and more important to a society undergoing profound and accelerated change, the feminisation of the teaching profession is a significant international phenomenon which deserves study. How women exercise their roles within the teaching profession has many implications attached to it. The authors of this study have made a signal contribution to our understanding of the facts and issues involved in the contemporary Irish context. They raise significant policy issues which should engage the attention of all stakeholders as we plan for our education system into the new century.

From the analysis of trends in some other European countries it is clear that the Irish experience of women exercising leadership positions is largely in line with such trends. The research literature indicates that there is considerable commonality at work in the social forces, processes of appointment and personal attitudes which contribute to the gender imbalance which is so prevalent. One of the difficulties which faced the authors in their study of the Irish situation was the inadequacy of the database which has existed relating to the teaching force. While the full picture is still incomplete, this book provides the most comprehensive set of relevant data published to date. The data establish that the feminisation of the teaching profession is accelerating in all four sectors studied – primary, secondary, community and comprehensive and vocational sectors. The process at primary level is such that if current trends continue men will only form a very small minority of the teaching force in that sector. Interestingly, the two sectors which hitherto had the best gender balance – community and comprehensive and vocational – are shown to be changing rapidly in recent years.

However, when it comes to patterns of promotion, there is a striking contrast, with women being in the minority in all sectors. It might have been expected that with the decline in religious sisters in positions of leadership that lay women would have more posts available to them. Instead, the authors record "With the decrease in the proportion of women in administrative principalships at primary level and of women principals in secondary schools, it appears that men are being appointed to a proportion of the positions hitherto held by religious sisters". Rationalisation of school provision is also favouring men teachers, particularly in co-educational schools. Much interesting data emerge from the study of patterns in each sector, as for instance, the finding that the number of women in administrative principalships in primary schools has dropped by almost a fifth since 1986.

The authors conduct a valuable exploration of women's attitudes in relation to promotion issues. Among reasons for a relatively low level of female applications for senior positions are: the pressure of caring work; the value that women place on family life; the lack of role models and peers in management; the problem of mobility; and the limited number of options open to women. However, there are also perceived structural barriers that discourage women from applying and aspects of power relations which act as discouragement, as well as the composition of selection committees. Change of attitudes by all stakeholders is seen as crucial in bringing about change in the proportion of women in school leadership. To help attitude change among women themselves, the authors point to the success of a pilot programme on women in management sponsored by the Department of Education and Science, a model that seems to hold promise.

The final chapter of the book contains a concise and very focused summary of the key findings of the study. It goes on to set out a range of recommendations under three headings: collection of data and research, planning for equality, and resources for support structures for principals.

The issues raised in the volume deserve public attention and efforts need to be made to remove all unfair barriers which may exist inhibiting the promotion of women teachers, while respecting each woman's right to opt out of leadership posts, some of which can be very stressful, in favour of other values she may hold. It is interesting to note that the Northern Ireland Ministry of Education has recently published a companion research volume, *Women in Teaching: Equal Opportunities*. Our Department of Education and Science deserves credit for commissioning this study of experience in this state. It has also commissioned a research study on imbalance in male and female entrants to primary teacher education colleges, which will be available shortly. Thus, we will have research data, information and proposals for action, which hold much promise for future policy in redressing the serious and growing imbalance in the career structure of women teachers in Ireland.

Women teachers, lay and clerical, have contributed enormously to Irish schooling over the last two centuries. In the context of accelerating social and educational change and significant new developments affecting the teaching profession for the future, such as the proposed establishment of a Teaching Council, it is essential that structures and supports are put in place to facilitate women taking their appropriate place in leadership positions in our schools for the new century.

LIST OF TABLES

Table 2.1: Women as a percentage of primary teachers and primary principals, in selected countries of Europe 15

Table 2.2: Women as a percentage of second-level teachers and second-level principals, selected countries of Europe... 16

Table 3.1: Women as a percentage of teachers in primary and second-level schools in Ireland.. 26

Table 3.2: Women as a percentage of all primary teachers and of primary teachers under the age of 30 at two points in time, 1976 and 1996 27

Table 3.3: Women as a percentage of teachers under 30 and as a percentage of teachers on the ten lowest points of the salary scale, in each second-level sector, 1996 27

Table 3.4: Numbers and percentages of women and men over the age of 50 in each sector and on the lowest ten points of salary scale, in three second-level sectors, in 1996.. 32

Table 3.5a: Selected age groups of primary teachers in 1976, 1986 and 1996 35

Table 3.5b: Selected age groups of primary teachers in 1986 and 1996 36

Table 3.6: Selected age groups of secondary teachers, 1985 and 1995 38

Table 3.7a: Community & comprehensive schools: percentage of women by age and point on salary scale, 1996 42

Table 3.7b: Community & comprehensive schools: percentage of men by age and point on salary scale, 1996 43

Table 3.8a: The vocational sector: percentage of women by age and point on salary scale, 1996 46

Table 3.8b: The vocational sector: percentage of men by age and point on salary scale, 1996 47

Table 4.1: Women in promotional posts relative to the percentage of women in each sector, 1996 54

Table 4.2: Women as a percentage of principals and vice-principals in secondary schools 55

Table 4.3: Types of primary principals by gender, 1976, 1986 and 1996 60

Table 4.4: Promotional posts in primary schools, by age cohort and gender, 1996 62

Table 4.5: Vice-principalships in secondary schools by age cohort and gender, 1996 65

Table 4.6: Teachers in all promoted posts and in senior positions (principalships, vice-principalships and A posts) in community & comprehensive schools by gender and age group, 1996 67

Table 4.7: Teachers in all promoted posts and in senior positions (principalships, vice-principalships and A posts) in the vocational sector by gender and age group, 1996 69

Table 4.8: Applicants and newly appointed principals in primary schools by gender over three separate periods of two years 71

Table 4.9 Percentages of applications and appointments to posts of responsibility in community & comprehensive schools, by gender, 1993-96 72

Table 4.10: Applications and appointments for posts of responsibility in the vocational sector, by gender, 1993-96 75

Table 4.11: Application rates for posts of responsibility in vocational schools, as a percentage of the number of eligible teachers, by gender, 1993-96 75

LIST OF FIGURES

Figure 2.1: Looking at career strategies 13

Figure 3.1: The percentage of primary teachers in each age group by gender, 1996 28

Figure 3.2: The percentage of women and men by point on the salary scale in secondary schools, 1996 29

Figure 3.3: The percentage of women and men by point of the salary scale in community & comprehensive schools, 1996 30

Figure 3.4: The percentage of women and men by point on the salary scale in the vocational sector, 1996 31

Figure 4.1: Women as a percentage of teachers in promotional posts in vocational schools, 1985/86 and 1996 58

Chapter 1

INTRODUCTION

Profound changes have taken place in the Irish education system in the past 20 years and continue apace. These include the rationalisation of schools from single sex to coeducational and from small to larger institutions, changes in management structures, particularly the change-over from religious to lay principals in primary and secondary schools and the setting up of Boards of Management in all sectors (Government of Ireland, 1998). Alongside these changes, a process of feminisation is taking place across all first and second-level sectors. However, while women form the majority of teachers in first and second-level education in Ireland, they are not present in the same proportions in the decision-making areas of education, in particular the management of schools (Lynch, 1997).

Furthermore, as the demographic structure of the country changes, the trend in Irish education is towards the rationalisation and amalgamation of schools into co-educational schools (ASTI Convention Reports, 1988-1996). Women have only been appointed to approximately 20 per cent of principalships in co-educational secondary and in community & comprehensive schools (Warren, 1997; Lynch, 1999). If this pattern continues and if a similar pattern emerges in the case of amalgamations of schools, then the proportion of women principals will decline in the immediate future.

The low level of applications by women for management positions is an issue that has been discussed in previous research and has been put forward as a reason for the lack of women in management in schools (Kellaghan and Fontes, 1985). The proportion of female applicants for principalships has been reported as around 20 per cent in community & comprehensive schools, while in the secondary sector the proportion of women applying for principalships appears to be very low overall, less than ten per cent (Lynch, 1997).

It is important that women play a full role in all aspects of the education system for a number of reasons. First, it is important that young people, boys and girls, see that women can command public positions of authority and influence. Secondly, if women do not play their full role in these positions, leaders will be chosen from far less than half of the teaching body, and the leadership potential of women will be lost to schools. Thirdly, in order to facilitate the personal development of women in schools, it is important that limits are not placed on their career development by barriers to promotion and/or misplaced reticence on their part. It is considered that women in education will become more "invisible", unless some action is taken to counteract current trends.

An effective strategy cannot be planned unless the processes within the system are understood as far as possible. Heretofore, the figures available both on the applications for and the appointment to principalship were inadequate and lacking in detail. This study was designed to correct the inadequacies in the data available and to come to a fuller understanding of the position of women in the education system.

The objectives of this research were therefore centred on gathering data relating to women in educational management and furthering the analysis of the underlying pressures which are influencing current changes in the organisation and management of schools. The specific objectives were:

- To compare the position of women in schools in Ireland with that of their counterparts in other European countries, in an analysis of current changes.

- To explore possible reasons for the current gender imbalance in the management of schools through a review of the research literature.

- To extend and deepen the knowledge in the public sphere with regard to women in educational management in primary and second-level schools, in particular, the evidence of differences in career patterns of women and men, the position of women in educational management in the primary, secondary, community & comprehensive and vocational sectors and the pattern of application to different levels of promotion in schools.

- To explore women's attitudes and values in relation to leadership in education and thus deepen the analysis of the pressures related to their low rate of applications for senior positions.

OUTLINE OF FURTHER CHAPTERS

Chapter 2 examines the context in which this study is placed, the literature on women in educational management. This includes an analysis of how the situation in Ireland compares with that of other European countries.

Chapter 3 presents an analysis of the structure of the teaching body at first and second level, including the rate of feminisation and career patterns of men and women in teaching.

Chapter 4 presents data on aspects of gender and promotion in primary and second-level schools, including applications and appointments to promotional posts in the vocational and community & comprehensive sectors.

Chapter 5 presents an analysis of career blocks that affect women in the system and some evidence of women's attitudes towards and perceptions of issues related to careers in education in Ireland.

Chapter 6 gives an account of the design and piloting of a leadership development programme for women from primary and second-level sectors, as an example of a positive intervention strategy.

Chapter 7 presents conclusions and recommendations.

The lack of gender balance in educational leadership and management is manifest across Europe and to a growing extent in Ireland. The female voice is being lost in educational management as a low proportion of women is appointed to principalship. A key issue appears to be the lack of applications from women for positions in management. This study addresses the question as to why such a pattern exists. It explores the increasing gender imbalance in education and analyses recent changes in the area of promotion and women in education. Finally, it identifies possible strategic interventions to encourage women to play an increasing role in educational management and to step "out of the shadows" (Blackmore, 1993).

Notes for Readers

For the purposes of this research, school types are divided into four sectors: primary, secondary (sometimes referred to as "voluntary secondary"), community & comprehensive and the vocational sector which includes vocational schools and community colleges. The community & comprehensive schools are grouped into one sector, as they are similar in structure and are associated with one management representative body, the Association of Community & Comprehensive Schools (ACS).

This research is based on data gathered as part of a project commissioned by the Equality Committee of the Department of Education and Science. The publication of this book is supported by that committee.

Chapter 2

THE CONTEXT

INTRODUCTION

The overall aim of this study is to deepen and clarify the understanding of the changing role and position of women and men in the Irish education system. The context is a time when schools are undergoing rationalisation and amalgamation, and when religious congregations are withdrawing from the direct management of primary and secondary schools and are appointing principals from among the lay teaching body. In this process, men, to a considerable extent, are replacing the religious in the management function so that a fundamental shift in the gender balance in management is taking place. As the majority of Irish second-level schools are in the secondary sector, this process has a major impact on the management and leadership of schools.

The theoretical approach to the research on women in educational management has varied over the years. This chapter outlines the different approaches, explores a number of theories on women's career development and examines figures relating to women in educational management in a number of European countries, comparing them with the situation in Ireland. The final part of the chapter looks at issues that have emerged in the literature in relation to how inequalities in educational management develop: the social construction of inequality in educational management and leadership.

RESEARCH IN EDUCATIONAL MANAGEMENT: THEORETICAL APPROACHES

There is a considerable body of research literature on the topic of women in education and in educational management, which now spans almost three decades. Many of the researchers have not given an indication of their philosophical approach but a pattern of change over time is clear. Blackmore (1993) outlines how the nature of teaching and educational administration has been theorised to fit the sexual divisions of labour, so that the developing situation where women teach and men manage can be viewed as the "natural order" and unproblematic. This describes the non-feminist approach. Two of the main types of feminist theories may be identified in more recent educational research: liberal feminism and radical feminism (Acker, 1983; Weiner, 1994). Those who espouse liberal feminism generally aim to establish equality of opportunity, not necessarily equality of outcome. There are some important criticisms of this theoretical approach, chiefly that it accepts current structures where the majority of women remain in subordinate positions and allows a few token women to have careers (Acker, 1994). This approach allows the argument that once overt barriers have been removed, any further differences in representation in management are due to the free choices or lack of ability of women (Shakeshaft, 1989). The contribution of research from this perspective has been to provide basic data relating to the position of women and men in educational management.

In radical feminism, on the other hand, the goal is not just equality of opportunity and of access but perhaps equality of outcomes. The contribution of research from this perspective has been to attempt to analyse power relations in organisations and the impact of such power relations on the overall structure (Weiner, 1994). This approach challenges the previous assumptions that women's lack of representation in management is due to lack of interest and analyses the development of the current situation in terms of the impact of androcentric structures on the careers of women. The research literature is reviewed here for the insight each perspective gives to the development of thought in this area.

The Non-feminist Approach

In a critique of sociological work on women and teaching, Acker highlighted the non-feminist approach of some sociologists of the 1950s and 1960s (Acker, 1983). Her main criticism was of the "blame the victim" approach which she identified in the work of Simpson and Simpson on the "semi-professions" (Simpson and Simpson, 1969, quoted in Acker, 1983). Their contention was that women are less committed to their work than men, less likely to maintain a high level of specialised knowledge, more willing to accept bureaucratic controls and, in essence, that the presence of women harms the status of the professions they occupy. Others such as Leggatt (1970) referred to women's "typical" characteristics of submissiveness and lack of ambition. Acker reviewed other later work which showed greater awareness of sexual divisions and greater empathy towards the career aspirations of women, such as Lortie (1975), Lacey (1977) and Hilsum and Start (1974). Despite this awareness, however, Lortie stopped short of a realisation that the "flat" career which he described as the lot of teachers was much more true for women teachers. Acker (1983) focused on and criticised the underlying assumptions in these pieces of research, some of which were:

- A deficit model of women, or a "blame the victim" approach. This asserted that women typically lack confidence, ambition and commitment.

- A tendency to see women primarily in terms of family roles. Discussion on women's careers tended to focus on married women as though all women teachers were married, whereas the marital status of men is not mentioned in discussion on careers.

- A simplified view of the causes of sexual divisions in educational careers.

Liberal Feminism and Research

The gender imbalance in education was highlighted as liberal feminism developed as an accepted theoretical approach in sociology, and some researchers focused on women in education as a subject. An example of one such piece of research in Ireland was a study by Kellaghan and Fontes (1985), which identified a number of barriers that appeared to block the career development of women. These included: lack of experience of teaching the full range of year groups, breaks in career, all male interview boards, and lack of childcare facilities. The recommendations of the report focused on methods to overcome these barriers and commented on the need to change the attitudes of teachers themselves regarding women's caring role in the home. One of the major conclusions was that more men are appointed to principalships because they apply in greater numbers. The deeper reasons why women do not apply were not dealt with in the research. This was in keeping with the liberal feminist approach which highlighted barriers in law or in custom and practice and the aim was the removal of such barriers. The response from those who control entry into management positions, the "gatekeepers",[1] may fit into this theoretical approach: that women are not appointed to principalships because they do not apply for the positions in great enough numbers or because they must be unsuitable and/or incompetent (Shakeshaft, 1989).

Radical Feminism and Research

As the limitations of liberal feminism as an instrument of analysis became clear, the development of radical feminism challenged the assumptions and predictions of this approach. Shakeshaft (1989) suggested that barriers labelled as internal by other researchers can also be seen as masking deeper societal barriers. She suggested, for instance, that the low confidence of women might be viewed as a product of a system in which women cannot gain experience in the areas of work which would boost their confidence.

The radical feminist perspective was also used to cast a different light on other issues such as women's low aspirations. The assumption that women have lower aspirations was based on male descriptions of career aspiration, namely, to aspire to become a manager and leave the classroom. However, women's commonly

---

[1] The term "gatekeeper" is used to refer to those who have power in the promotion processes, i.e. those who sit on selection committees or whose recommendation is considered important for promotion.

held career aspiration, to become an excellent teacher, had not been considered in the discussion of career development. A number of studies have shown that women enter teaching in order to teach and that this motivation is stronger for women than for men (Gross and Trask, 1976; Kellaghan and Fontes, 1985).

Other researchers have also challenged the liberal feminist analysis. Adkison (1981) pointed out that research in the United States indicated that women were preparing for leadership positions in education through education and training. Research further showed that many of those women seeking management positions did not conform to sex role stereotypes but showed ambition for promotion, confidence in their ability and assertiveness. During the same period, however, despite the increase in interest and level of training of women for management in education, the proportion of women in principalships and assistant principalships declined. Adkison's conclusion was that the response of the organisations needed to be examined to ascertain possible reasons for women's lack of success.

Other radical feminist researchers examined the issue of power and relationships within organisations as related to gender, in particular Kanter (1977). Her ethnography of a large multinational corporation examined how the organisational structures served to limit the success of women in gaining access to positions of power. Kanter identified a number of areas in which the norms of behaviour within the organisation operated to limit the opportunities for women:

- The senior management group depended on a high level of trust in order to function, hence homogeneity was important. Thus the gatekeepers tended to appoint candidates who fitted in with the management group, which was all male.

- Women and others who did not fit into the senior management style or culture tended to be promoted, if at all, to positions which were outside the main decision-making group.

- A woman who was promoted to a senior position became a "token" woman with the associated problems identified by Kanter: the token is seen as representing her group (all women), and as being typical of women; is highly visible so that mistakes are highlighted but is invisible and silenced when attempting to voice an unpopular opinion.

Cockburn (1991) identified a variety of ways in which the culture of the workplace creates an environment in which women do not flourish. The "chill factor" makes it clear that women are out of place in management, and "successful women are made targets for a lot of hostility and comment" (Cockburn, 1991, p. 67). O'Connor (1998) also identified the organisational culture of a number of Health Boards in Ireland as a factor that created barriers to promotion for women. Cockburn (1991) identified how women who reached higher managerial positions were encouraged to be more masculine and yet these same women were then held up as negative role models for younger women to discourage them from seeking promotion. Thus women are set against each other within the organisation. The overall effect is to limit the power and influence of those women who reach management positions and discourage more junior women from developing career ambitions. Hill and Ragland (1995) outlined a range of similar findings in educational settings. They commented that women report either being ignored or interrupted when attempting to contribute to important discussions, or in some instances being dismissed through the assumption that they were not really responsible for a particular successful project or decision.

Shakeshaft (1989) and Ouston (1993) highlighted how career socialisation research has focused on the process of informal role-learning before appointment, in the form of anticipatory socialisation. The candidate seeks opportunities to learn and demonstrate administrative skills. If successful, the candidate may be appointed to committees, or may be afforded training opportunities. A number of researchers in education have concluded that such socialisation is more difficult for women (Shakeshaft, 1989; Ouston, 1993) making the transition from teaching to administration particularly difficult for them, as they are then competing for positions against men who have had these opportunities.

Adkison reported further research which argued that the informal system of rewards in school can be very important: who attends conferences, who represents the school at meetings, who is nominated for leadership training and who receives direct communication from the principal. Ball (1987) highlighted how women as a special interest group on a teaching staff may be controlled through the micro-political activity among the staff, by overt sanctions or by a range of apparently insignificant social interactions: overt sexist remarks, making senior women the butt of jokes and interruptions of women's contributions to discussions. Cunnison (1989) also discussed the male-female balance of power and how verbal and non-verbal behaviours may be used to control women: joking, particularly about senior women, comments on appearance and dress, positive or negative, as a means of highlighting a woman's sexuality, the use of anger and a range of non-verbal controlling behaviours. Buchan (1980) observed, summarising the impact of the range of micro-political behaviours on women teachers:

> There are numerous overt and covert pressures designed to encourage women to step gracefully aside and let men move up the ladder (Buchan, 1980, p. 87).

Thus, research into the lack of women in educational management has changed in focus over time and as different feminist and other theoretical perspectives developed. Some research ignored the role of women or focused on the "problems" associated with them such as their lack of ambition, lack of commitment, or their negative influence on the status of their profession. The liberal feminist approach highlighted overt barriers to women's promotion but tended to focus only on the overt causes. The research using the radical feminist perspective has attempted to explore more deep-seated reasons for women's lack of representation in management in education, focusing on power relations in organisations and the social pressures that affect the careers of women.

WOMEN'S CAREER DEVELOPMENT

While the underlying perspective in research in this area has changed over time, certain key issues have been highlighted as having an influence on the development of women's careers in education. One important development has been the recognition that the theory of career development had not hitherto taken account of the experiences of women, but had developed within an androcentric paradigm (Larwood and Gutek, 1987). Recent theories provide a structure in which women's career aspirations, choices and outcomes can begin to be analysed and unnecessary career blocks removed.

The work of Evetts (1990 and 1994) on career development suggests a structure in which the career choices of women teachers can be examined. Evetts initially outlined five types of career histories which she suggested would best describe the careers of women. At a later stage, she developed a theory based on a study of career strategies in which both men and women can be accommodated and which can be used to conceptualise the process of career development. The following is a combination of the two concepts.

Evetts categorised one type of situation as the "one person, one career" type. This was a single person in a demanding career, with no partner or children. This category tended to be occupied by single women. The "two persons, one career" was exclusively a man in a demanding career with a woman working full-time in caring work in the home, or in a job with no opportunities for promotion or not seeking promotion. Evetts noted that while men who used this strategy had been promoted to a principalship at an early stage, the single women achieved early promotion to middle management level but then had to wait a longer time to reach a principalship (Evetts, 1994).

For a person whose spouse is pursuing a demanding career, and who is thus in a situation of "two persons, one career", teaching is possibly used as a job with limited opportunities for promotion. Teachers who are in such a position and who do not seek promotion were described by Evetts in 1990 as in "accommodated careers" and they tended to be women. There are other teachers who would have different reasons to remain in teaching without seeking promotion, who would also be described as "accommodated", such as those who prefer classroom teaching to administration, or those who value their lifestyle as teachers and hence do not seek promotion. If a teacher who is in this position later changes their mind and seeks promotion, Evetts (1990) classified this as a subsequent career.

In the "dual career" situation, which Evetts (1994) defined as a household where both career interests receive equal status, three successful strategies were identified, postponement, modification and balancing. In the postponement strategy, one person held back and at a later stage took steps to develop a career. In Evetts study (1994) it was exclusively women who did this. She noted that this strategy is more likely to lead to modest promotional achievements, but that it worked well for those who used it and were happy in it. Evetts was, of course, dealing with principal teachers. There may be many dissatisfied teachers who used this strategy and were not so successful. The modification and balancing strategies were used when partners attempted to develop careers simultaneously. They involved major career changes or partners making career moves alternately. These can be difficult to achieve and it was the failure of such strategies that partially led to the marital breakdown referred to in two cases in Evetts' study (1994).

FIGURE 2.1: LOOKING AT CAREER STRATEGIES

Single Career	One person	A single person who single-mindedly pursues a career
	Two person	a) spouse a homemaker b) spouse in job with few opportunities, who does not seek promotion
Dual Career	Postponement Strategy	Empty nest syndrome: spouse develops a subsequent career; may be planned or a response to circumstances
	Modification Strategy	Change in career to accommodate spouse
	Balancing Strategy	Both careers developed
Marital Breakdown		As a result of a failure of career strategies

After Evetts, 1990 and 1994

White (1995) also examined successful women's careers from a feminist viewpoint. Forty-eight women who were judged by their peers to have developed successful careers were interviewed. While White argued that clear career stages would no longer hold for women or men in the workplace of the future, certain phases in the lives of these women emerged. A pattern emerged of periods of relative stability followed by periods of change. One of the common periods of change related to women making decisions with regard to children. The majority of these successful women had postponed having a family until their thirties. A second common period of dissonance occurred at a later stage when a reassessment of these choices caused tension or when the "glass ceiling" or a block to further career development was encountered.

The work of Evetts and White highlights the concept of career as a response to changing life circumstances. The theory of women's career development must be considered in the context of all aspects of women's lives. In attempting to understand the paths that women in particular may take, it is important to consider the life choices as well as the career choices open to them.

THE EUROPEAN DIMENSION

An important aspect of the context of this study is the position of women in education and in educational management in other European countries and in particular the identification of changes in the gender balance of management in education, similar to the Irish situation.

Throughout Europe, teaching at primary level is highly feminised, with women forming almost three quarters of the teaching force in all but two countries, Belgium and Greece (Table 2.1). Ireland lies midway in this list of eleven countries in terms of the degree of feminisation. Men occupy the majority of principalships in all but two countries (Table 2.1): France, where the percentage of women principals stands at 64 per cent compared with the 79 per cent of teachers who are women (Fave-Bonnet, 1997), and Portugal, where 90 per cent of principals are women, almost equal to the 91 per cent of teachers who are women (Laemers and Ruijs,' 1996). Ireland again lies in the middle range of the countries listed here when proportions of women teachers and principals are compared.

The relationship between the percentage of teachers and principals who are women is considerably worse in the Netherlands than in any of the other countries listed. The background factors leading to such gender imbalance in the Netherlands are complex, including the introduction of coeducational schools in the 1970s with a resulting loss of women principals, the replacement of principals who were religious sisters[2] by men and the amalgamations of infant and primary schools from 1985 onwards, in which two thirds of women lost their principalships compared with one tenth of men (Vermeulen and Ruijs, 1997).

TABLE 2.1: WOMEN AS A PERCENTAGE OF PRIMARY TEACHERS AND PRIMARY PRINCIPALS, IN SELECTED COUNTRIES OF EUROPE

Country	Teachers	Principals	Ratio T/P
Italy	93	46	2.0
Portugal*	91	90	1.0
Hungary	85	33	2.6
UK	81	49	1.7
France	79	64	1.2
Ireland	78	46	1.7
Netherlands	76	13	5.8
Spain	74	47	1.6
Norway	74	40	1.9
Belgium*	62	39	1.6
Greece	50	41	1.2

After Wilson 1997b and Laemers and Ruijs, 1996*. Irish figures include religious sisters.

At second level, the feminisation of the profession is less marked. In more than half of the countries presented in Table 2.2, there is a gender balance with women representing between 40 and 60 per cent of teachers. In a number of countries, including Ireland, however, the proportion of women at second level is increasing, for example, in Italy (Campani and Picciolini, 1997) and in Greece (Kontogiannopoulou-Polydorides and Zambeta, 1997).

---

[2] In this study the term "religious sisters" has been used throughout to refer to women who are members of religious congregations.

TABLE 2.2: WOMEN AS A PERCENTAGE OF SECOND-LEVEL TEACHERS AND SECOND-LEVEL PRINCIPALS, SELECTED COUNTRIES OF EUROPE

Country	Teachers	Principals	Ratio T/P
Hungary	97	30	3.2
Portugal*	71	23	3.1
Italy	63	30	2.1
France	56	30	1.9
Ireland	54	29	1.9
Greece	53	36	1.5
Belgium*	50	28	1.8
Spain	50	20	2.5
UK	49	26	1.9
Norway*	39	22	1.8
Netherlands	33	7	4.7

After Wilson, 1997b and Laemers and Ruijs, 1996*. Irish figures include religious sisters.

The proportion of women principals is lower at second level than at primary level, falling between seven per cent in the Netherlands and a high of 36 per cent in Greece. In Portugal there is a considerable contrast in the proportion of women principals at second level compared with primary level. Whereas at primary level there is parity and the ratio of the percentage of women principals to teachers is 1:1, at second level, the ratio is 1:3.1, the third most unbalanced of the European countries listed. In the case of the Netherlands, the education system at second level and as already discussed at primary level, has gone through a process similar to that which is now developing in Ireland. In the 1960s and 1970s single sex schools were amalgamated to form coeducational schools. At the same time, religious sisters who had been managing and teaching in the single sex girls' schools withdrew from them. The result was a drop in women principals from 11 per cent in 1978-79 to four per cent in 1988, followed by a rise to the present figure of seven per cent (Vermeulen and Ruijs, 1997). While the proportion of women principals is much less overall, this situation is similar to that evolving in Ireland today. The education system at second level in Ireland is in a process of change as two thirds of the 54 per cent of principals who are women are religious sisters (Lynch, 1999). A greater gender imbalance is likely to develop as these religious sisters are replaced by lay principals, particularly as the record to date shows that almost 40 per cent of principals appointed in single sex girls' schools in the period 1991 to 1995 were men (ASTI, 1995). The gender imbalance that is already in evidence in Ireland is therefore likely to increase.

In countries across Europe, women are more likely to be principals of schools for younger children, for instance in infant schools in the Netherlands before the amalgamations of the 1980s (Vermeulen and Ruijs, 1997), and in primary rather than second-level schools in all the countries represented in Tables 2.1 and 2.2. They are also more likely to hold principalships in situations where the principal has to teach as well as act as principal, as in Norway (Oftedal, 1997), and France (Fave-Bonnet, 1997), and in smaller schools rather than large urban schools as in Norway. This is in contrast with the pattern of women finding it easier to gain management positions in urban areas in the United States (Shakeshaft, 1989).

INEQUALITY IN EDUCATIONAL MANAGEMENT: CONTRIBUTING FACTORS

In the research literature a number of issues have emerged highlighting the interaction of a complex web of influences on the current position of women in management. These include the extra responsibility of caring work coupled with a lack of mobility for women, the impact of socialisation on their careers and career plans, and finally, the conceptualisation of management (Coldron and Boulton, 1998).

Responsibilities and Mobility

Childcare and home responsibilities have been identified as issues for women considering seeking promotion (Diamond, 1987). Women carry the greater workload in these areas (Coldron and Boulton, 1998; Moran, 1993). Pregnancy and responsibility for the care of children and others have a direct effect on women's attitudes and values. Women tend to develop their career only if they are satisfied that it will not adversely affect their partner and children (Evetts, 1990; Mullarkey, 1994).

Associated with family responsibilities, there can be a lack of mobility if a career move for a woman involves moving home with spouse and children. Women are more likely to apply for promotion in their own school rather than another school or district (Grant, 1989; Mullarkey, 1994). The pattern of not applying to other schools may be related to this issue of mobility. It is likely that in teaching, more women than men are in dual career partnerships and their spouses tend to be earning more (Evetts, 1989; Moran, 1993). This has the potential effect of lessening women's mobility, as the spouse's career will probably take precedence. If a woman's spouse moves to further his career, this may lead to a mobility situation that disadvantages the female partner resulting in a break in service, loss of seniority and/or a difficulty in regaining a teaching position. The man's career is still generally seen as more important (Evetts, 1989; Kellaghan and Fontes, 1985). This has implications not only for applications for promotion but also for women's career plans. In a situation where a woman is unsure if her future lies in one locality or another, it becomes impossible to plan a career or indeed to accept promotional positions that would involve long-term commitment. The low density of population in Ireland in comparison with other European countries and the resulting relatively sparse distribution of schools are also factors in career opportunities for women in education in this country, further exacerbating the problem of mobility. Women in education appear to be more conservative than women in business in this regard, or perhaps educational organisations are more conservative. A study of 35 women superintendents in the US reported that none had negotiated a job for her spouse so that she could move to a better position in a different location, while such a strategy is becoming relatively common in business (Hill and Ragland, 1995).

Socialisation and Women's Careers

There is evidence that women have a different approach to employment which has the effect of creating disadvantage for women seeking promotion. Women in particular seem to need encouragement in some form before they begin to consider a move into management, such as the experience of being managed by someone younger or less effective than themselves, or encouragement by a senior person in education whose opinion they respect (Gold, 1996). Research on women head teachers has concluded that women tend not to plan their career, as compared with men (Acker 1994; Adler *et al,* 1993). Indeed, the interaction between women's career development and other important aspects of their personal life as discussed earlier, makes it difficult for them to formulate definite career plans (White, 1995).

Other researchers have noted a difference in approach developing at an early stage between men and women in education. Gross and Trask (1976) reported that by the age of 25, 43 per cent of men and 13 per cent of women in teaching had considered a principalship as a goal. By the age of 30, the ratio was 35 per cent of women and 74 per cent of men. In a study by Grant (1987), few of the 38 women deputy heads in the study had started with a definite career plan. Ouston (1993) noted that women may have career goals but make *ad hoc* arrangements to achieve them. It is evident that women have a different approach to career, which does not involve setting goals for advancement at an early stage.

Those who are thinking of moving into management begin to look at themselves in a different way and begin to see themselves as potential leaders, the career socialisation process discussed by Adkison (1981). The opportunity to try out leadership roles, or to become visible in the school as a possible leader are key steps in the career socialisation process. Adkison (1981) contends that such career preparation opportunities are more available to men than to women. Such experience can be crucial in developing self-knowledge, confidence, a mentoring relationship and other supports and skills. Research indicates that women who are promoted to satisfy quotas without the opportunity to develop skills in this way are more likely to fail in the job (ibid). The opportunity to develop a relationship with a more senior person (a mentor) is a key aspect of this process. A mentor could provide critical information about political realities, techniques to deal with bureaucracy, ways to deal with budgets and other essential survival techniques (Hill and Ragland, 1995). Women appear to have more difficulty than men in acquiring such a mentor.

Related to the difficulty in finding a mentor is the issue of career positioning. Poor career positioning has been put forward as an explanation of the lack of promotion for women (Hill and Ragland, 1995), while Ball (1987) notes that women may be marginalised because of their lack of political awareness. O'Connor (1998, p. 240) used the term "organisational naiveté" to describe a similar phenomenon in Health Boards in Ireland. Hill and Ragland note that:

> ... women lack a sense of how people receive advancements in their organisations. They are conditioned to think that hard work, good performance and adding to their competence will necessarily allow them to advance (Hill and Ragland, 1995, p. 76).

The lack of role models in positions of authority has been pointed to as an important factor in the reluctance of women to apply for promotion to principalships (Shakeshaft, 1989). The fact that in Ireland there have been ample role models for women in single sex girls' schools, as the majority of principals have been religious sisters in the past, has not been explored. The rate of applications from women for principalships in these schools appears to have been higher than in other second-level schools (Warren, 1997) but there has been no research as yet into the micro-politics of such schools, or the effects, if any, of the presence of a principal who is a woman and a religious sister, as a role model.

Lack of peers who are being promoted is possibly as important as the lack of mentors or role models in seeking an understanding of the career attitudes of women. It has been noted that men grow increasingly anxious to be at the appropriate level of career development when they see their peers being promoted (Grant, 1989). Women, however, tend to use other women as a reference group for a comparison with their own career progress, particularly when in a female dominated profession. The result is that women report satisfaction with their own promotion even when they acknowledge that women in general are discriminated against (Zanna, *et al,* 1987). Kanter (1977) found that workers who were in low opportunity positions tended to become less concerned with promotion and more concerned with interpersonal relationships at work. Marshall (1984) noted that women have been forced to adapt to limited opportunities by becoming job-oriented, rather than career-oriented.

It has been recognised that there are distinctly different patterns of application rates from men and women for promotion (Ozga, 1993; O'Hara, 1994). Women are less likely to apply repeatedly for promotion. Ouston (1993) noted that while equal proportions of men and women had applied for a promotion over two years, many more men had applied for more than four promotions. The pattern of lack of persistence in applying could be explained by a noted lack of self-confidence in women and a tendency to explain failure in terms of personal lack of self-worth rather than external factors (Shakeshaft, 1993). Thus men blame external factors when they are not promoted and continue to apply for other posts. Women, on the other hand, are much more likely to believe that the reason they were not successful was because they were not good enough, and hence stop applying.

The Conceptualisation of Management

The image that women teachers have of the management process could be an important influence on their perception of how they would "fit" the job, and their inclination to seek such a position. Theories of management and leadership have tended to be developed from a male perspective, with initial research not considering women subjects because of the absence of women managers and an underlying assumption that the male experience is universal (Blackmore, 1993; Shakeshaft, 1989). Evetts (1989) concludes that the masculine image of management leads to problems for women in how they act as managers. The image of management as demonstrated by many principals is not compelling to women. They may reject aspects of management such as aggressive competitive behaviours, an emphasis on control rather than negotiation and a competitive rather than collaborative approach to problem solving, which some may find repugnant and dysfunctional (Al-Khalifa, 1989). Dunlap (1995) noted that women who had decided not to seek leadership roles viewed the models of leadership that surrounded them as the only models available, and considered these models unsuited to their preferred style of leadership. In facilitating training courses for women, Gold (1994) found that the definition of management that emerges from all-women groups is quite different from that produced by mixed-sex groups. The women's groups define management in more collaborative terms, with less emphasis on control. Women who have been appointed to principalships and who seek to develop a leadership style which is outside the traditional male norm can have difficulty and may initially be challenged by the staff more than men in managerial positions would tend to be (Shakeshaft, 1989). Hall (1996) however, argues that management in schools has a different quality because it also involves leadership. In a close analysis of the leadership styles of six women principals, Hall concluded that each had reinterpreted management and the use of power to include leadership and empowerment of others.

The difficulty experienced by some women managers in conceptualising and using a different style of management may also be an issue in the attitudes and ideas of those making management appointments. Alimo-Metcalfe (1995) in a survey of attitudes of senior managers found a divergence in the perception of men and women, of the qualities needed for leadership. Alimo-Metcalfe found that men in this group tended to hold views of management qualities that were very much in keeping with values of "good management" in the traditional style. If the gatekeepers or the members of selection committees have an image of management that is traditional and hierarchical, this has obvious implications for possible discrimination in the process of appointments. There appears to be a continuing problem in Ireland of gender imbalance on interview boards and women experiencing questions which indicate that the interviewers hold such an image (Daly, 1989; O'Hara, 1994).

Thus, a more collaborative participative style of management that has been termed a "feminine" style of management has been explored in recent years in the literature (Gray, 1987; Al-Khalifa, 1989; Shakeshaft, 1989; Ouston, 1993; Gold, 1994, 1996; and Hall, 1996). Gold (1994) however, points out that defining management styles as "male" or "female" is too rigid and does not allow for growth and change in managers. She and Evans have developed the concept of this type of management as a reflective style of management (Gold and Evans, 1998). While this reflective, collaborative style of management is now recognised as more successful in schools (Fullan, 1991) it may not translate into reality without difficulty. Alimo-Metcalfe (1995) noted that the language of empowerment may be used without the philosophy, leading to manipulation as "empowerment". Kanter, however, formed the view that a new organisational form, which is more collaborative and in which women can move from tokenism to participation, is in evidence (Kanter, 1991). This style of management and leadership is not in evidence in some schools in Ireland, where a controlling adversarial style of management still operates (Gibbons, 1996).

SUMMARY

Research on the lack of women in educational management and on women's careers in teaching has been carried out from different theoretical perspectives. The liberal feminist approach identified barriers to women's advancement but the analysis tended to be limited to the superficial reasons for women's lack of progress. Radical feminist research has identified a range of other explanations, focusing on power relations in schools and in the system that limit the career aspirations of women in education. Women's career choices are made in the context of their personal lives and values so that the "traditional" career path is not always possible for, or attractive to, women.

The pattern of feminisation of primary teaching in Ireland along with a gender imbalance in management is mirrored in many other European countries. Some of the developments that have exacerbated the gender imbalance in other countries are part of the current process of change here, in particular, rationalisation to co-educational and larger schools.

While the situation in Ireland in second-level education appears relatively balanced in terms of gender compared with some other European countries, the fact that two-thirds of women principals are religious sisters is a factor that signals changes to come. In the Netherlands, in a similar situation, the percentage of women principals fell by almost two-thirds in a decade.

A variety of pressures have been identified as important in reducing the rate of application for promotion among women teachers, including issues related to the workplace and to women's own personal lives. These include the difficulties women may have in planning a career related to caring work and the resulting loss of mobility, a different approach to career planning that may have the effect of creating disadvantage for women, an "organisational naiveté" in women's approach to career positioning which coincides with a lack of mentors, role models and peers on promotional paths, and conflicting concepts of management and leadership.

The traditional directive and controlling style of management appears not to suit the majority of women who tend to aspire to a more collaborative style. While it has been argued that this more democratic style is a more effective style of management, women may experience difficulty in putting this into practice and may be challenged more by staff. The attitudes and views of the gatekeepers are also important in this regard as the evidence suggests that those in a position to participate in making appointments may have the traditional view of management as a male construct.

The issues outlined above provide the context for an in-depth analysis of the current structure of the teaching profession in Ireland and the changing place of women in it.

Chapter 3

THE TEACHING CAREER: FINDINGS AND ANALYSIS

INTRODUCTION

An important consideration in first and second-level education is the changing gender balance of the teaching body, the influence of which has been considered to date only at primary level (INTO, 1995). In this chapter, gender balance is examined in the context of the process of change that is occurring in first and second-level education, along with a discussion of the career continuity patterns and the career trajectories of teachers.

Analysis of career patterns in teaching in Ireland has been hampered by the limited availability of data. The figures gathered for this study add to the level of information available but the picture remains incomplete and at times is not comparable across sectors. Appendix 1 gives an account of the process by which the data was gathered. Due to the lack of information available on teachers in temporary or part-time positions, only teachers in permanent incremental positions are considered in this analysis.

In the case of the primary and secondary sectors, an analysis of the teaching body at three points in time over a 20-year period is presented. In the community & comprehensive and vocational sectors, longitudinal data was not available but a detailed analysis of the teaching body by age, gender and point on salary scale is presented. This gives evidence of aspects of the career trajectories of teachers in these sectors.

THE FEMINISATION OF THE TEACHING PROFESSION

A process of feminisation is evident in both first and second-level education, in that the greater proportion of teachers employed are female. Three aspects of the process are examined here: the overall pattern of feminisation, the feminisation process in each sector and the rate of feminisation.

The Overall Pattern of Feminisation

At primary level, the process of feminisation had already progressed to a large degree but recent change is now evident also in the three sectors at second level. Table 3.1 presents the figures for 1996 compared with data previously published (Drudy and Lynch, 1993). The proportion of women has increased in all sectors.

TABLE 3.1: WOMEN AS A PERCENTAGE OF TEACHERS IN PRIMARY AND SECOND-LEVEL SCHOOLS IN IRELAND

	Previous Data*		1996**
School Type	**Year**	**% Women**	**% Women**
Primary	1976	71.3	77.7
Secondary	1993	55.0	58.4
Community & Comprehensive	1993	46.0	50.0
Vocational	1986	41.2	50.0

Sources: *Drudy and Lynch, 1993; ** Department of Education and Science.

While there appears to be a gender balance in vocational and community & comprehensive sectors, with 50 per cent women in each sector, the proportion of women is increasing in these sectors over time (Table 3.1).

In order to examine the rate of change, the data available for each sector is further analysed. At second level, the proportion of men and women at each point of the salary scale was available. This data was not available at primary level. However, the total number of men and women in each age group over a 20-year period was available and illustrates the feminisation process. The proportion of teachers who were women in the teaching body as a whole and of those under 30 years of age in 1976 and 1996 at primary level is shown in Table 3.2.

TABLE 3.2: WOMEN AS A PERCENTAGE OF ALL PRIMARY TEACHERS AND OF PRIMARY TEACHERS UNDER THE AGE OF 30 AT TWO POINTS IN TIME, 1976 AND 1996

	1976	1996
Women as a % of all primary teachers	71.3	77.7
Women as a % of primary teachers under 30 years of age	70.3	84.4

Source: Department of Education and Science.

The high and growing proportion of women in this sector is evident from Table 3.2. Women currently form 84.4 per cent of teachers who are under 30, indicating a process of feminisation much further advanced than in any of the second-level sectors, as is the pattern in other European countries (Chapter 2).

TABLE 3.3: WOMEN AS A PERCENTAGE OF TEACHERS UNDER 30 AND AS A PERCENTAGE OF TEACHERS ON THE TEN LOWEST POINTS OF THE SALARY SCALE, IN EACH SECOND-LEVEL SECTOR, 1996

	Secondary	Community & Comprehensive	Vocational
Women as a % of teachers under 30 years of age	92.5	94.6	75.0
Women as a % of teachers on lowest 10 points of salary scale	73.4	67.2	71.4

Sources: Department of Education and Science, individual community & comprehensive schools and Vocational Education Committees.

At second level, data on the teaching body by age group and position on the salary scale highlights the extent to which the process of feminisation is ongoing in all three sectors (Table 3.3). The younger teachers in these sectors are predominantly women, the proportions being 93 per cent, 95 per cent and 75 per cent of those under 30 in each of the sectors respectively (Table 3.3). The balance of men and women among recent recruits, teachers on the lowest ten points of the salary scale,[1] however, is quite different. The proportions then change to 74 per cent, 67 per cent and 71 per cent respectively. These figures indicate that younger men are absent from teaching compared with women and thus, that men tend to begin their teaching career at a later age than do women in some sectors. In the following section, each sector is examined to clarify the changes taking place.

The Feminisation Process: The Primary Sector

Data on the proportion of men and women on each point of the salary scale is not available for this sector, so age is used as an indicator of the feminisation process. In 1993/94, 86.6 per cent of students in Colleges of Education were women while by 1996/97, this had risen to 88.9 per cent (Ruane and Sutherland, 1999). This is reflected in the percentage of men in the age group 20 to 24, that is, 10.1 per cent (Figure 3.1).

FIGURE 3.1: THE PERCENTAGE OF PRIMARY TEACHERS IN EACH AGE GROUP BY GENDER, 1996

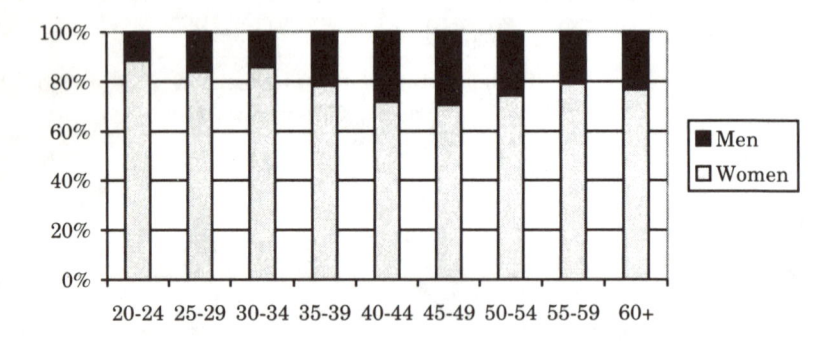

Source: Department of Education and Science.

It is notable that the decline in the number of men is not a smooth progression through the age groups. There are variations in the gender balance, with the highest proportion of men in the age cohort 45 to 49. This is examined further below. The trend towards

---

[1] Each teacher in a permanent position progresses up the salary scale to the 26th point.

feminisation of the teaching profession at primary level is evident in the age groups 20 to 24 and 25 to 29. In these groups it is progressing to the point where men will be a very small minority in the primary sector if current trends continue.

The Feminisation Process: The Secondary Sector

In the three sectors at second level, data on the proportion of women and men at each point of the salary scale has been gathered, as well as data on the age structure of teachers and this is examined here. A number of important aspects of the salary scale for teachers should be noted. First, the majority of teachers, those who hold a primary degree, begin on the third point of the salary scale. Secondly, it is not possible to "skip" points on the scale or to be appointed to begin on a higher point unless a teacher has been in a "temporary wholetime" position prior to a permanent appointment. How this would affect the overall figures is difficult to ascertain.

The overall gender balance of teachers on each point of the salary scale in secondary schools is clear in Figure 3.2: men form the majority at the 26th point, the top of the salary scale, women at all other points.

FIGURE 3.2: THE PERCENTAGE OF WOMEN AND MEN BY POINT ON THE SALARY SCALE IN SECONDARY SCHOOLS, 1996

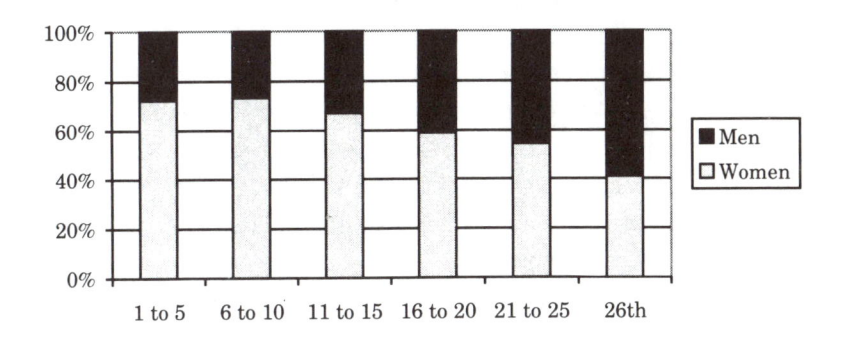

Source: Department of Education and Science

The proportion of women on salary scales one to five and six to ten is over 70 per cent and it falls gradually as the point on the scale increases, to a low of 41 per cent on the 26th point. There is a higher proportion of teachers on the 26th point of the salary scale than on any of the other points since it is possible to reach that point in the age group 45 to 49 and remain there until retirement, usually at the age of 60 to 65[2].

The Feminisation Process: The Community & Comprehensive Sector

The proportion of women and men at each point of the salary scale in this sector is shown in Figure 3.3.

FIGURE 3.3: THE PERCENTAGE OF WOMEN AND MEN BY POINT OF THE SALARY SCALE IN COMMUNITY & COMPREHENSIVE SCHOOLS, 1996

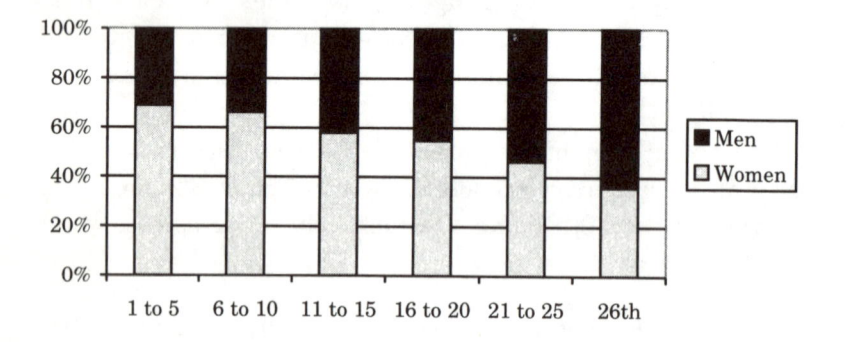

Source: Community & comprehensive schools

There is a greater predominance of men on the top point of the salary scale in this sector than in the secondary sectors, although this sector is only in existence since the late 1960s. This indicates that more older men than women were drawn into these schools from other sectors, perhaps when these schools were being set up, or perhaps as a result of school amalgamation. The proportion of teachers who are women is lower in each group than is the case in secondary schools. Men are still in a minority at all points below the 21st point on the salary scale.

---

[2] There was no provision for retirement with pension in second-level education at an earlier age prior to an agreement under the Programme for Competitiveness and Work, 1998, unless on grounds of ill-health.

The Feminisation Process: The Vocational Sector

The rate of change in the balance of women and men in this sector is shown in Figure 3.4.

FIGURE 3.4: THE PERCENTAGE OF WOMEN AND MEN BY POINT ON THE SALARY SCALE IN THE VOCATIONAL SECTOR, 1996

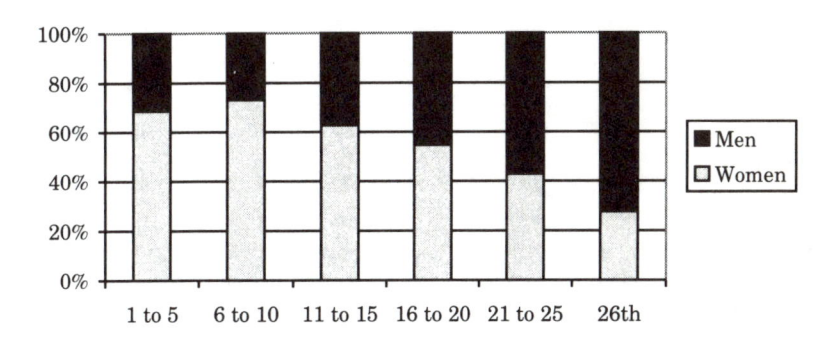

Source: Vocational Education Committees

The very high proportion of men at the top point of the salary scale, point 26, and the high proportion of women at the lower end of the salary scale indicates that there is rapid change underway in this sector. This rate of change is set to continue for two reasons. First, the high proportion of men on point 26 and above of the salary scale, will mean a higher proportion of men than women leaving due to retirement. Secondly, the high proportion of women on the lower points of the salary scale indicates a recruitment pattern that is quite different to that of the past. This point is explored further below.

The Rate of Feminisation

The rate of feminisation over the next ten to 15 years will be decided by the proportion of women and men who are retiring in that time, compared with the number of women and men being recruited into the different sectors. Figures for the numbers and gender balance of teachers over 50 years of age in four sectors are presented in the first half of Table 3.4. Figures showing recent recruitment of teachers onto the first ten points of the salary scale for the three second-level sectors are also presented in Table 3.4. Data for the primary sector is not available by salary scale.

TABLE 3.4: NUMBERS AND PERCENTAGES OF WOMEN AND MEN OVER THE AGE OF 50 IN EACH SECTOR AND ON THE LOWEST TEN POINTS OF SALARY SCALE, IN THREE SECOND-LEVEL SECTORS, IN 1996

Sector	Teachers Over 50 Years of Age		Teachers on Lowest 10 Points of Salary Scale		Total	
	% Women	% Men	% Women	% Men	% Women	% Men
Primary	76.5	23.5	n/a	n/a	77.7	22.2
Secondary	47.5	52.5	73.4	26.6	58.4	41.6
Community & Comp	33.7	66.3	67.2	32.8	50.0	50.0
Vocational	16.6	83.4	71.7	28.3	50.0	50.0

Sources: Department of Education and Science, individual community & comprehensive schools and Vocational Education Committees.

The figure for those under 30 years of age in the primary sector, 84.4 per cent (Table 3.2) indicates that there is change occurring in that sector, although the gender balance of those over 50 and the teaching body as a whole indicates that this increase is occurring slowly. In the secondary sector, the gender balance of recent recruits indicates an increase in the proportion of women: on the lower points of the scale, the proportion of women is over 70 per cent. The overall gender balance in the community & comprehensive and vocational sectors masks an imbalance in the structure of the teaching body in those sectors. The high proportion of men in the older age groups balanced the high proportion of women on the ten lowest points of the salary scale. These sectors are now showing the greatest rate of change because of these same factors: a high proportion of men over the age of 50 combined with a high recruitment rate for women.

The rate of change is different in the four sectors and it is accelerated by the high proportion of men in the over 50 age group in the community & comprehensive and vocational sectors. It is evident that the vocational sector, which has had the highest proportion of men in the recent past, is experiencing the fastest rate of feminisation.

CAREER CONTINUITY AND DISCONTINUITY

While the feminisation of the teaching profession is evident from the above data, the pattern of career continuity for teachers, men and women, has not been examined in any detail heretofore. This issue has a potentially important influence on promotions in teaching. Both the rate at which women break their careers and the extent to which women lose career time because of breaks for child-bearing and child-rearing have been noted in the research as having a negative influence on promotional opportunities for women (Chapter 2).

In order to examine this issue, data was gathered in relation to the age and gender profile of the teaching body where possible. In the case of two sectors this data was available for the teaching body over a period of time. In the primary sector, details of the numbers of men and women teachers in different age groups were made available by the Department of Education and Science for 1976, 1986 and 1996, allowing a comparison of career trajectories over a 20-year period. This data is presented and discussed below. At second level, comparable data was available only for secondary teachers and then only for the years 1985 and 1995. The data does not represent a longitudinal study of a distinct group of teachers, strictly speaking, as any number of entries and exits may be hidden in the figures. One is, however, broadly examining the same age cohorts over time. The figures presented here for these sectors are termed longitudinal profiles of the teaching body.

In the vocational and community & comprehensive sectors the data available was limited to the structure of the teaching body in the year 1996. However, details of the age and position of men and women on the salary scale in these two sectors allowed an exploration by gender of the phenomenon of discontinuity in teaching careers or late entry into teaching. The question that is addressed is whether women and men are on the point of the salary scale based on expected entry age and a continuous career in teaching.

PROFILES OF THE TEACHING BODY:
PRIMARY AND SECONDARY SECTORS

The data available in these sectors allows a comparison of the same groups of teachers over a period of 20 years in the primary sector and over a period of ten years in the secondary sector, giving an indication of trends in these two sectors. A caveat must be entered here in relation to the interpretation of the data in this section. Teachers who are on career break (available since the mid-1980s), or who are job sharing, or who are employed on a part-time or temporary basis are not included in the data. There is also no data on teachers who change from one sector to another or who move in and out of the system. Notwithstanding this, the analysis highlights important issues relating to the career trajectories of teachers.

In Table 3.5a and Table 3.5b (the primary sector) and Table 3.6 (the secondary sector), a number of cohorts of teachers are compared with the same group 20 and ten years later respectively. For example, in Table 3.5a, teacher numbers in the age group 20 to 24 in 1976 are compared with the numbers in the age group 30 to 34 in 1986 and in the age group 40 to 44 in 1996. Thus, corresponding cohorts of teachers are compared over a period of 20 years in order to ascertain the degree to which there is evidence of changes in continuity in teachers' careers over time and the differences by gender.

Profile of the Teaching Body: The Primary Sector

As the marriage bar was abolished in the primary sector in 1956, women who may have been affected by the requirement to retire on marriage had almost all left the system by 1996. Newly qualified teachers in 1956 (aged 19 or more) would be 59 years of age or more by 1996. The rate of continuity in participation in the primary sector could therefore be expected to be similar for men and women, in the absence of a legal requirement for women to retire on marriage. The data presented in Table 3.5a indicates considerable gender differences in career participation patterns, and changes in these patterns over the two ten-year periods presented in the table.

TABLE 3.5A: SELECTED AGE GROUPS OF PRIMARY TEACHERS, 1976, 1986 AND 1996.

Age in			Women			Men		
1976	1986	1996	Number in 1976	1986 figure as % of 1976	1996 figure as % of 1986	Number in 1976	1986 figure as % of 1976	1996 figure as % of 1986
20-24	30-34	40-44	2386	+17.1	-1.3	957	+20.3	-4.6
25-29	35-39	45-49	1982	-2.3	+0.3	892	-3.4	-6.3
30-34	40-44	50-54	1613	+3.0	-3.8	617	-3.1	-7.7
35-39	45-49	55-59	1710	+2.5	-11.1	519	-3.7	-23.4
40-44	50-54	60-64	1380	-1.2	-54.1	494	-7.1	-58.2

Source: Department of Education and Science

The predominance of women in this sector discussed above is evident in Table 3.5a. Three further trends evident in the table are discussed here. A fairly high proportion of men and women are entering the profession late, over the age of 25. This is evident for women and men who were in the age group 20 to 24 in 1976. Both of these groups increased in number in the decade to 1986: by 17 per cent and 21 per cent respectively. Table 3.5b presents comparable data for the younger age cohorts who have joined the teaching profession since 1976 in this sector.

TABLE 3.5B: SELECTED AGE GROUPS OF PRIMARY TEACHERS IN 1986 AND 1996

Age in		Number in 1986		% Increase or Decrease by 1996	
1986	*1996*	*Women*	*Men*	*Women*	*Men*
20-24	30-34	2,232	370	+24.4	+26.5
25-29	35-39	2,955	765	−9.6	−3.1

Source: Department of Education and Science

In the age group 20 to 24 in 1986, the same trend is evident, with both men and women showing an increase of around 25 per cent of the 1986 figure in the ten years to 1996. An exploration of the factors that may be leading to this late entry to the profession by both men and women is beyond the scope of this work and remains a question for future research.

There is little evidence in Figure 3.5b of women losing career time in that each cohort remains relatively close to the original figure. This may, of course, mask a flow of women out of the teaching body and a balancing flow returning. The age group aged 25 to 29 in 1976 shows a small decline by 1986 and a small increase in the period 1986 to 1996, evidence for some movement in and out of the teaching body that may be related to women taking time out of their career for child-minding. Other cohorts also show very small changes. One cohort in Table 3.5b shows a fall in the number of women. The cohort aged 25 to 29 in 1986 show a decrease of ten per cent by 1996. As career breaks of up to five years were introduced in the mid-1980s, it appears that this represents the response of women to the opportunity to take time out for family or other reasons. For other age groups, there is no evidence in this data for significant loss of career time for women in the primary sector.

The third trend evident in Table 3.5a relates to the loss of men from the profession throughout the 20-year period. After an initial gain for late entries that is comparable with the gain for women, men show a continuous loss in each age group over each ten-year period, which is greater than the loss of women in each cohort (Table 3.5a). The exception to this is the cohort aged 25 to 29 in 1986 in Table 3.5b, where the loss of men is just above three per cent compared with almost ten per cent of women. This is a relatively small difference in career patterns. It appears that this pattern of men leaving teaching is an increasing trend, as the losses for the decade 1986 to 1996 are greater than the corresponding losses in the period 1976 to 1986 (Table 3.5a).

These findings must be interpreted with the caveat that they show patterns of overall numbers but there is no control for teachers who enter the profession late, those who interrupted their career, or those who are currently on a career break or job sharing. Similarly, a number of institutional changes may have had an impact on these figures, such as the rate of recruitment to permanent teaching positions as a result of changes in the pupil/teacher ratio, demographic changes and the introduction of career breaks in the 1980s. The impact of these cannot be explored further at present. Notwithstanding these limitations, the trends are clear that it is men who tend to leave teaching rather than women and that there is little evidence for loss of career time on the part of women with the exception of the age cohort aged 25 to 29 (in 1986). These findings suggest areas for more focused and/or qualitative research on the career trajectories of teachers.

Profile of the Teaching Body: The Secondary Sector

Table 3.6 shows similar data for teachers in the secondary sector, for the years 1985 and 1995. The age groups over 55 in 1986 are excluded, as are those under 30 in 1995. The same caveat in the use of this data applies as to the primary sector, that there is no evidence of the rate of flow of teachers into or out of the sector which would have a direct bearing on the data in the table.

TABLE 3.6: SELECTED AGE GROUPS OF SECONDARY TEACHERS, 1985 AND 1995

Age in		Number in 1985		% Increase or Decrease by 1995	
1985	1995	Women	Men	Women	Men
20-24	30-34	333	156	+258.0	+473.7
25-29	35-39	1520	849	-13.8	-9.0
30-34	40-44	1522	1123	-12.4	-9.7
35-39	45-49	972	1194	+4.3	-11.5
40-44	50-54	650	836	-7.5	-6.0
45-49	55-59	506	590	-21.3	-10.7
50-54	60-64	386	323	-50.5	-38.1

Source: Department of Education and Science

Similar trends are evident in the secondary sector in Table 3.6 as in the primary sector. The changing gender balance through the age groups is evident, as discussed above. A number of other trends are discussed here. The late entry to the profession is also evident in the figures, showing the increase in the cohort aged 20 to 24 in 1985 for both men and women by 1995. The very high proportion of secondary teachers who are not appointed to a permanent incremental position until the age of 25 and over is a continuing trend first identified by Drudy and Lynch (1993). Younger teachers are spending some years as part-time or substitute teachers before securing a permanent appointment. The greater increase in the numbers of men, approaching 500 per cent in 1995, compared with just over 250 per cent for women, indicates a late entry into teaching for a higher proportion of men than women in this sector. Drudy and Lynch (1993), however, found that more men than women tended to have greater success in securing permanent teaching positions on completion of the Higher Diploma in Education. This, along with the data presented above, points to a pattern of men not choosing a career in teaching until a later age than women. This gender difference is not evident in the primary sector (Table 3.5a above).

The second trend evident in Table 3.6 is the loss of women in the age groups 25 to 29 and 30 to 34. It appears that women leave the profession in this sector either temporarily or permanently in the age groups 25 to 29 and 30 to 34 in 1985. As in the primary sector, the introduction of career breaks may have influenced this trend. The loss in teacher numbers is comparable with the primary sector for the age group 25 to 29 in 1985 (a drop of almost ten per cent in 1986, Table 3.5) but is greater than the decrease for the age group 30 to 34 in 1986 (9.7 per cent in the secondary sector compared with under 2 per cent in the primary sector). Whether this represents women leaving their career for full-time caring work in the home or for other careers in education or elsewhere, remains a question to be addressed in further research. In contrast, there is an increase in numbers in the age group 35 to 39 (in 1985) in the ten years to 1995 of four per cent. It appears reasonable to suggest that this may represent women returning to teaching when children are grown but it could also represent women starting a career at this stage.

The trend of persistent loss of men from all age cohorts in the secondary sector evident in Table 3.6 is similar to that in the primary sector. While a higher proportion of women leave in the age groups 25 to 29 and 30 to 34, for men there is a consistent loss in all age groups from 25 upwards.

Compared with the figures for the primary sector, the loss of men in the three age cohorts 25 to 29, 30 to 34 and 35 to 39 is much greater in the secondary sector, indicating a movement of a considerable proportion of men out of teaching or at least out of this sector of education. The lower percentage of men leaving teaching in the higher age groups (–38.1 per cent) compared with the primary sector (–58.2 per cent), may be due to the fact that the minimum retirement age (with pension) in this sector before 1998 was 60 years of age compared with 55 in the primary sector. The loss of men out of secondary teaching may represent a movement to other sectors in education, or to other careers in education, or a movement out of education to other careers. A contributing factor may be the movement of male members of religious congregations out of the education system. It is an issue that is beyond the scope of this study but indicates patterns of career trajectories for men in teaching that have not been heretofore identified or discussed.

CAREER CONTINUITY AND DISCONTINUITY IN THE COMMUNITY & COMPREHENSIVE AND VOCATIONAL SECTORS

This section analyses the structure of the teaching body with regard to continuity of career for men and women in two sectors, the community & comprehensive and the vocational sectors. In the absence of data over a period of ten or 20 years, the figures available for one year, 1996, are used to examine career continuity patterns among the current body of teachers in these sectors. The position of teachers on the salary scale in comparison with their age is examined. Loss of career time due to late starts and/or one or more career breaks is then evident.

Method of Presentation of Data

A working assumption was made that a teacher who had entered third level at the usual age of 17 to 19 and entered the teaching profession immediately on qualification would be on one of the points one to five of the salary scale up to the age of 24. It should be noted that those who hold a degree and teaching qualification start on the third point of the salary scale. Appendix 2 includes a table in which the data for women teachers in secondary schools is set out and shaded to indicate the method of construction of the following tables, Tables 3.7a, 3.7b, 3.8a and 3.8b.

Following the assumption that those aged 20 to 24 would be expected to be on points one to five of the salary scale, those aged 25 to 29 would be expected to be on points six to ten of the salary scale, those aged 30 to 34 on points 11 to 15 of the salary scale, and so on. The percentage of teachers in each age cohort on the expected points of the salary scale is represented in the column "Expected point on salary scale". Those teachers who were ahead of their age group, i.e., teachers aged 24 or under who were on points six to ten of the salary scale and so on up the age cohorts, were designated as "earlier than expected". Those teachers who were further down the salary scale than expected were designated as "delayed" in their career.

Teachers on point 26, the top of the salary scale, include those who have been on that point for some years and those who have just reached it. These teachers may be early in their career, on time, or late by up to 16 years in the case of the age group 60 to 65. This limits the usefulness of the data for teachers at the top of the scale, in the age groups 50 to 54 and upwards, who are shown in Tables 3.7a, 3.7b, 3.8a and 3.8b as "On expected point". This also means that the data for careers delayed is not discernible for these age groups unless they are delayed by a considerable number of years. Those parts of Tables 3.7a, 3.7b, 3.8a and 3.8b in which the figures are limited in this way have been shaded in the tables to indicate this.

In discussion of careers in teaching, a number of caveats must be considered. First, there is no evidence in relation to continuity of career within an individual school or within a sector: indeed there is free movement between the three second-level sectors. Secondly, the interpretation of delays in careers must be treated with care as such a delay may be the result of a late start, a break in career, a temporary transfer to another profession, or a series of breaks in career. Only in the instances where teachers are on the lowest five points of the salary scale at a relatively advanced age can it be stated with certainty that this represents a late start in the teaching career. Thirdly, variations in the rate of appointments to permanent positions have occurred over recent decades, due to education cutbacks or demographic changes (Drudy and Lynch, 1993). Nevertheless, important gender differences are evident.

Career Continuity and Discontinuity in the Community & Comprehensive Sector

The breakdown of the teaching body in this sector by age highlights the differences in the age structure of women and men, outlined in the discussion on the feminisation of this sector. The other gender differences include, as in the secondary sector, a delayed entry to the teaching career, which is a greater phenomenon for men than for women, and gender differences in loss of career time through all age groups.

TABLE 3.7A: COMMUNITY & COMPREHENSIVE SCHOOLS: PERCENTAGE OF WOMEN BY AGE AND POINT ON SALARY SCALE, 1996

Age Group	Expected Point on Salary Scale	% of Women on Higher than Expected Point on Salary Scale	% of Women on Expected Point on Salary Scale	% of Women Showing Loss of Career Time by Number of Years Lost				Total (n)	Age Group as % of Total
				1-5	6-10	11-15	16+		
20-24	1-5	1.6	98.4					61	4.2
25-29	6-10	0.5	58.5	41.0				183	12.6
30-34	11-15	4.1	14.4	47.1	7.4			244	16.7
35-39	16-20	9.4	46.2	36.8	6.6	1.0		288	19.7
40-44	21-25	0.6	46.7	37.8	7.4	5.7	1.8	336	23.0
45-49	26		22.4	46.3	20.1	6.7	4.5	134	9.2
50-54	26		62.3		22.6	12.3	2.8	106	7.3
55-59	26		73.6			12.5	13.9	72	4.9
60-65	26		85.7				14.3	35	2.4
Total		2.8	50.5	33.2	7.8	3.6	2.1	1,459	

Source: Community & comprehensive schools. Shading indicates limitations on data (see text). One school missing.

TABLE 3.7B: COMMUNITY & COMPREHENSIVE SCHOOLS: PERCENTAGE OF MEN BY AGE AND POINT ON SALARY SCALE, 1996

Age Group	Expected Point on Salary Scale	% of Men on Higher than Expected Point on Salary Scale	% of Men on Expected Point on Salary Scale	% of Men Showing Loss of Career Time by Number of Years Lost				Total (n)	Age Group as % of Total
				1-5	6-10	11-15	16+		
20-24	1-5	0.0	0.0					0	0.0
25-29	6-10	0.0	7.1	92.9				14	1.0
30-34	11-15	2.2	30.4	44.3	23.1			230	15.5
35-39	16-20	9.7	46.5	35.0	8.4	0.4		226	15.2
40-44	21-25	0.7	48.1	41.1	5.9	3.5	0.7	287	19.3
45-49	26		47.3	41.1	7.5	2.2	1.9	319	21.5
50-54	26		84.0		10.8	3.5	1.7	231	15.5
55-59	26		88.0			6.0	6.0	117	7.9
60-65	26		93.3				6.7	60	4.1
Total		2.0	55.0	29.9	9.3	2.2	1.6	1,486	

Source: Community & comprehensive schools. Shading indicates limitations on data (see text). One school missing.

The proportion of men and women in the different age groups shows considerable variation. In particular, it is notable that none of the teachers under 25 are men, an indication that the same pattern of a late start to a teaching career for men as found in the secondary sector applies here. Thus, one-third of women teachers are under 35 in this sector, compared with a quarter of men. In the older age groups, less than a quarter of women are over 45, compared with almost half of men in this sector (Tables 3.7a and 3.7b).

The loss of career time is indicated in the section of Tables 3.7a and 3.7b labeled "% of women/men showing loss of career time by number of years lost". As a result of the difference in career starting age, it is notable that while 60 per cent of women under 30 are "on the expected point" of the salary scale, only seven per cent of men in this group are in a similar position.

As career discontinuity may have implications for the promotion opportunities of teachers, the focus here is on losses of more than six years of career time through a late start or career breaks. There are considerable gender differences by age groups to be observed in this regard. Up to the age of 39, the teaching careers of a higher proportion of men show a delay of more than six years. This is particularly evident in the age group 30 to 34, where almost a quarter of men are in this position compared with only seven per cent of women. In the age groups 40 to 44 and 45 to 49, the trend is reversed, with women showing a greater loss of career time. The greatest difference is in the age group 45 to 49 where almost one third of women have lost more than six years of career time compared with just over 11 per cent of men. In the age groups over 50, as indicated above, the figures are less useful. It is notable, however, that a greater proportion of women have lost a considerable amount of time when compared with men in these age groups.

Career Continuity and Discontinuity in the Vocational Sector

The difference in the age structure of men and women in this sector is significant, as highlighted in the section above on the feminisation of teaching. This is the only second-level sector with men under 25 years of age. However, the proportion of men under 35 is very low, at 13 per cent compared with one third of women. The proportion of the women and men over 45 years of age reflects what was discussed above with regard to the rate of feminisation. Twenty-eight per cent of women are over 45 years, compared with 57 per cent of men.

There is no evidence of the phenomenon of men entering teaching later than women in this sector, as the proportion of men and women starting late is very similar in the age groups 20 to 24 and 25 to 29. This raises questions that are beyond the scope of this research, as to why men appear to enter teaching later than women in the other two second-level sectors and not in this sector.

In this sector, career patterns for men and women are more similar than in the community & comprehensive sector. It must be noted, however, that the proportion of teachers over 50 years of age who are women is low in comparison with the proportion of men. Whether women were recruited originally in these age cohorts and left the profession subsequently, or whether they were not recruited at all remains a question that cannot be answered using the data available to date.

There is evidence of a loss of career time for women in the age group 30 to 34 with over half delayed by one to five years (Table 3.8.a). The equivalent figure for men is 44 per cent (Table 3.8.b) but in this age group, more men than women have lost between six and ten years, nine per cent and seven per cent respectively. This loss of time may represent career discontinuity or a late entry to the profession in both cases. In the age group 35 to 39 a higher proportion of women, (50 per cent), are on the expected point of the salary scale or higher, while the figure for men is considerably lower at 42 per cent. While a higher proportion of women have lost more than six years in this age group, the difference between men and women is not great, 13 per cent and 14 per cent respectively. Similarly, in the age group 45 to 49, men and women have similar patterns but again a higher proportion of women have lost more than six years, just over a quarter of women compared with 14 per cent of men. This appears to be an increasing trend for older teachers, as in the age group 50 to 54 the figures are 27 per cent for women and 19 per cent for men. Above that age group the data is incomplete as discussed above, but it is evident that a relatively high proportion of women in the upper age groups have lost a considerable number of years of career time.

TABLE 3.8A: THE VOCATIONAL SECTOR: PERCENTAGE OF WOMEN BY AGE AND POINT ON SALARY SCALE, 1996

Age Group	Expected Point on Salary Scale	% of Women on Higher than Expected Point on Salary Scale	% of Women on Expected Point on Salary Scale	% of Women Showing Loss of Career Time by Number of Years Lost				Total (n)	Age Group as % of Total
				1-5	6-10	11-15	16+		
20-24	1-5	5.5	94.5					55	2.1
25-29	6-10	4.4	61.0	34.6				367	13.8
30-34	11-15	2.2	38.4	52.8	6.6			453	17.1
35-39	16-20	2.7	48.0	35.0	12.2	2.1		515	19.4
40-44	21-25	1.9	40.0	41.2	9.6	5.2	2.1	522	19.2
45-49	26		36.4	38.1	11.2	8.2	6.1	376	14.2
50-54	26		73.0		7.7	11.2	8.2	196	7.4
55-59	26		68.8			14.7	16.5	109	4.1
60-65	26		70.0				30.0	60	2.3
Total		2.0	49.1	34.1	7.5	4.0	3.2	2,653	

Source: Vocational education committees. Shading indicates limitations on data (see text). One vocational education committee area missing.

TABLE 3.8B: THE VOCATIONAL SECTOR: PERCENTAGE OF MEN BY AGE AND POINT ON SALARY SCALE, 1996

Age Group	Expected Point on Salary Scale	% of Men on Higher than Expected Point on Salary Scale	% of Men on Expected Point on Salary Scale	% of Men Showing Loss of Career Time by Number of Years Lost				Total (n)	Age Group as % of Total
				1-5	6-10	11-15	16+		
20-24	1-5	0.0	100.0					12	0.5
25-29	6-10	0.8	55.0	44.2				129	4.8
30-34	11-15	0.0	46.1	44.7	9.2			217	8.1
35-39	16-20	0.4	41.5	45.4	8.5	4.3		282	10.6
40-44	21-25	1.2	39.7	49.8	6.3	2.4	0.6	506	19.0
45-49	26		42.7	43.5	11.4	1.0	1.4	588	22.1
50-54	26		80.9		13.8	2.8	2.6	509	19.1
55-59	26		92.1			3.6	4.3	278	10.4
60-65	26		93.8				6.3	144	5.4
Total		0.3	68.3	29.6	8.0	2.0	1.7	2,665	

Source: Vocational education committees. Shading indicates limitations on data (see text). One vocational education committee area missing.

SUMMARY

The data presented in this chapter highlights the extent to which the teaching profession is becoming more feminised in all sectors. Almost 85 per cent of primary teachers under 30 and 72 per cent of recent recruits in the secondary sector are women. The rate of change is particularly rapid in the two sectors that have traditionally had a higher proportion of men, the community & comprehensive and vocational sectors, where the proportion of women among recent recruits is 67 per cent and 71 per cent respectively.

A number of issues not documented hitherto have emerged in relation to the career patterns of men and women. In particular, the career trajectories of men in teaching do not follow the expected paths, with evidence of a late start and loss of men throughout their career in two sectors. There is evidence that women have lost career time in the past through breaks in career or late starts in the second-level sectors.

Feminisation

The process of feminisation is progressing in all four sectors of first and second-level education.

- The proportion of women in the younger age groups in the primary sector is in the region of 84 per cent and in colleges of education for primary teaching the proportion is almost 90 per cent. These figures indicate that feminisation is progressing in the primary sector.

- In the secondary sector the proportion of women is currently just over 58 per cent, a figure that indicates an upward trend compared with data published recently. Women form over 70 per cent of recent recruits, hence feminisation is also progressing in this sector.

- The rate of feminisation is most rapid in those sectors that traditionally had a higher proportion of men, namely the community & comprehensive and vocational sectors. These sectors show the greatest rate of change in the proportion of women teachers.

Longitudinal Data: Primary and Secondary Sectors

The data presented in this chapter allows a comparison of the same groups of teachers over a period of 20 years in the primary sector and over a period of ten years in the secondary sector, although without any evidence of flow of teachers into or out of these groups. The data gives an indication of trends in these two sectors. While there are limitations in how the figures can be interpreted, in particular because of the incomplete nature of the data, the analysis highlights important issues relating to the career trajectories of teachers.

- In the primary and secondary sectors, there is a trend for women and men to enter the profession relatively late. This is more pronounced in the secondary sector, where there is also a gender difference: a higher proportion of men enter late compared with women.

- Figures for the primary sector suggest that women have lost relatively little career time in the past. A recent trend shows a loss of almost ten per cent among women in their thirties, possibly as a result of women taking career breaks.

- In the secondary sector, there is evidence that about 14 per cent of women in their twenties leave the profession. There is a further loss of women in their early thirties. While these women may be leaving for family reasons, this may also represent movement between the three second-level sectors. There is evidence of an increase in the proportion of women in the age groups 35 to 39, suggesting a return after a short break or a very late entry to the profession.

- In both the primary and secondary sectors, there is evidence of men leaving the sector or the profession, throughout all age groups. In the primary sector, there is a persistent loss of men throughout the 20 years and it is an increasing trend. In the secondary sector, the only second-level sector where data of this kind was available, there is a greater flow of men out of the sector in the case of all age groups over 30. This may represent movement between sectors on the part of men, or movement out of teaching to other careers in education or elsewhere.

Loss of Career Time: Community & Comprehensive and Vocational Sectors

In these sectors the data analysed relates to the current body of teachers in one particular year, 1996. An analysis of the figures was done in relation to the age, gender and point on the salary scale of the teaching body. Allowing for the limitations of the information available for these sectors, the following trends are in evidence:

- In the community & comprehensive sector men begin their teaching career at a later age than women, but this trend is not in evidence in the vocational sector.

- In the community & comprehensive sector, it is men who show a loss of career time in the age groups under 40. Above that point, a higher proportion of women than men show greater loss of career time.

- In the vocational sector similar trends emerge, with both men and women showing loss of career time. It is in the older age groups that a distinct gender difference emerges, with higher proportions of women than men showing losses in excess of six years.

A number of issues have arisen in this chapter that would merit further research. First, the process of feminisation and its impact. Secondly, changes in women's career trajectories in the primary sector, in that women appear to be taking career breaks in their thirties. Thirdly, the late entry to teaching for men and women and in particular the gender differences in late entry in the secondary and community and comprehensive sectors. Fourthly, the persistent loss of men in the primary and secondary sectors, the only two sectors where adequate data was available to see that trend. There is a need for more complete data to be available on a regular basis so that such trends can be observed and their impact analysed.

Chapter 4

WOMEN AND PROMOTION: THE ROLE OF WOMEN TEACHERS IN SCHOOLS

INTRODUCTION

This study examines the processes which are currently influencing the gender imbalance in terms of promotion in the education system. The proportion of women in promotional positions in first and second level education in Ireland has been examined previously (Drudy and Lynch, 1993; Hannan and Smyth *et al*, 1996; Lynch, 1994, 1997 and 1999; Warren, 1997). Such studies have highlighted the low proportion of women in principalships and other promotion posts in schools in these sectors. Initially, this chapter examines anomalies in the promotional systems that were in existence prior to 1998. Following this, previous studies are updated and recent changes in the gender balance of promotion positions are examined. The analysis focuses on the interplay between issues such as the impact of rationalisation on the promotion of women, and the relationship between age, gender and promotion. The rate at which men and women apply for promotional posts is then examined, particularly in the community & comprehensive and vocational sectors, over a three-year period, 1993 to 1996.

ANOMALIES IN THE PROMOTION SYSTEM

There were a number of anomalies in the promotional system which have largely disappeared with recent changes in pay allowances for promotional positions.[1] The names of the promotional posts have also been changed,[2] but for the purposes of this study they are referred to by the titles used in 1996, the year when the data was gathered, namely, principal, vice-principal, A posts and B posts.

Since the data under discussion is from 1996, these anomalies existed at that time and are therefore examined here. Data on promotions in Irish schools has usually been presented in a particular hierarchy: principal, vice-principal, A post and B post. There is an underlying assumption that the principalship is the position with the highest status and salary, followed by the vice-principalship, then A post and finally B post. This has not always been the case, however. First, as the number and age of students were used in calculating the extra payments (allowances) for the principal and vice-principal, a principal or vice-principal in a small school may have been receiving an allowance lower than that of A or B post holder respectively. The assumption that a vice-principalship is a step up from an A post therefore may not always have held, at least in terms of salary. Similarly, a vice-principal in a large school would have been allocated an allowance greater than that of a principal in a smaller school with younger pupils. Therefore, these anomalies in the ranking of promotional posts must be borne in mind in the interpretation of the analysis which follows.

The Primary and Secondary Sectors

In the primary and secondary sectors, trade union/management agreements on promotions have had a particular impact on internal promotions. Before the 1998 agreement, promotional posts up to and including the level of vice-principal have been awarded on

---

[1] A national agreement on promotional posts in 1998 (under the Programme for Competitiveness and Work) changed the allowances and the system for calculating those allowances for the various positions. Age of pupils is no longer an important factor in calculating the allowances for principal and deputy principal.

[2] Since the 1998 agreement, the title principal remains as it was while the position of vice-principal has been replaced by deputy principal. In addition, A posts have been replaced by assistant principalships and B posts by special duties teacher.

the basis of seniority within the school.[3] This is no longer always the case for the position of vice-principal (now termed deputy principal).

Voluntary movement of a teacher from one school or sector to another leads to a loss of a promotional position, or loss of seniority for the individual teacher. This has contributed to a system in which there is little movement of teachers between schools except for movement to the position of principal, where that occurs. Thus, outside the large urban areas, there may be no promotional opportunities for teachers over a number of years. The relatively low density of population in Ireland means that distance between schools may be an issue in promotional opportunities. The aforementioned trade union/management agreement on promotions did not extend to the position of principal. Seniority is not a criterion in selection to that position and it is instead an appointment based on open competition following advertisements in the national newspapers.

Community & Comprehensive and Vocational Sectors

In the community & comprehensive and vocational sectors the system of appointment to all promotional posts was by open competition, with some exceptions. A union/management agreement was put in place in 1996 that set out a system of points to be allowed for criteria such as seniority in appointment to a certain proportion of A and B posts. While A posts have been appointed on an internal basis in primary, secondary and community & comprehensive schools, these have been advertised on a scheme-wide basis in the vocational sector. That is, A posts were advertised within the Vocational Education Committee area (Drudy and Lynch, 1993).

THE CURRENT SITUATION

The main point to emerge from the analysis of promotional posts is that women are under-represented in a range of promotional positions relative to the proportion of teachers who are women.

---

[3] Seniority was calculated on the basis of number of years spent teaching continuously in one school.

This is evident in relation to the position of principal in all sectors and to the positions of vice-principal and A post in all second-level sectors (Table 4.1). In addition, there is considerable variation in this trend across sectors.

Differences in the proportion of women in each promotional post are examined in terms of differences within the four sectors, differences across sectors and changes in recent years.

TABLE 4.1: WOMEN IN PROMOTIONAL POSTS RELATIVE TO THE PERCENTAGE OF WOMEN IN EACH SECTOR, 1996

	Primary	**Secondary**	**Community & Comp.**	**Vocational**
Principal	47.3	42.8	10.0	11.2
Vice-principal	82.9	40.9	22.2	22.8
A Posts	68.0	49.8	36.6	32.1
B Posts	76.2	54.0	50.0	47.4
% with no post who are women	85.0	65.9	57.2	67.6
% of total who are women	77.7	58.3	50.0	50.0

Sources: Department of Education and Science, individual community & comprehensive schools and Vocational Education Committees. One community school and one Vocational Education Committee area missing.

In the primary sector, the proportion of principals who are women is low in comparison with the proportion of teachers who are women. The ratio of teachers to principals who are women is 1.7:1. This appears to be balanced somewhat by the proportion of vice-principals who are women. This figure of 82.9 per cent is striking as it is the only position in which women are represented at a rate higher than the proportion of women in the teaching body as a whole. As discussed above, however, an unknown number of these vice-principalships would carry an allowance which would be the equivalent of an A or a B post. The proportion of women in A and B posts, at 68.0 and 76.2 per cent respectively, is slightly lower than the proportion of women in the teaching body as a whole (77.8 per cent). The proportion of women in these posts is likely to be due to the impact of a union/management agreement on promotion on the basis of seniority, as in the secondary sector (Drudy and Lynch, 1993). The proportion of women who do not hold a promotional post is considerably higher than the overall figure, at 85 per cent. This may reflect the higher proportions of young teachers who are women. The relationship between age and promotion is explored further below.

In the secondary sector, the proportion of principals who are women (42.8 per cent) is relatively high in comparison with the proportion of women in the sector (58.3 per cent). However, this represents a decrease since 1990/91 (Drudy and Lynch, 1993), which is discussed below. A further breakdown of the proportion of women in principalships in different school types within the secondary sector is not available at this time, but recent data from the National Survey on Coeducation indicates that there is considerable variation (Hannan and Smyth *et al*, 1996).

TABLE 4.2: WOMEN AS A PERCENTAGE OF PRINCIPALS AND VICE-PRINCIPALS IN SECONDARY SCHOOLS

	Single Sex Secondary		Coeducational
	Boys only	Girls only	
Mean % teachers: women	26	88	63
% principals: women	0	92	50
(of whom % religious sisters)	n/a	(67)	(80)
% vice-principals: women	0	77	35
No. of schools	18	26	20

Source: Hannan and Smyth *et al*, 1996.

This survey found that within the secondary sector, the proportion of principals who were women varied greatly by school type, from none in single sex boys' schools to 50 per cent in coeducational schools (of whom 80 per cent were religious sisters), to 92 per cent in single sex girls' schools.

It is notable that overall in the secondary sector, as in the other sectors and in other areas of the labour market, the lower the level of promotion, the higher the proportion of women. The system of promotion on the basis of seniority as outlined above has not resulted in promotion for women in proportion to their overall number in the sector. This proportion is approached in the case of the lowest promotional post, where 54 per cent of B post holders are women compared with 58.3 per cent of the total. This may be related to the trends outlined in Chapter 3 where women are in the majority in recent recruits and where a small number of women enter or re-enter teaching in their forties, as this would affect their seniority within the school.

In the community & comprehensive sector, the absence of any union/management agreement on promotion procedures has clearly had a negative effect on the representation of women in vice-principalships and A posts when compared with the primary and secondary sectors. As in the case of the secondary sector, the lower the level of promotion the higher the proportion of women. The proportion of women in B posts is equal to their representation in the body of teachers in this sector. It is in the position of principal, however, that the main imbalance is evident. The ratio of women teachers to women principals is 5:1. This means in effect that 90 per cent of principals are being appointed from 50 per cent of the teaching body.

In the vocational sector, the pattern of promotion of women is similar to that in the community & comprehensive sector, but with a lower proportion of women in A and B posts and a higher proportion of women with no post. This may be reflecting the greater proportion of women among recent recruits in this sector. This is discussed further below.

In a comparison across the four sectors the main point that emerges is the difference in the proportion of women in principalships and vice-principalships from a high of 47.3 per cent of principals and 82.9 per cent of vice-principals in the primary sector to a low of ten per cent and 22.2 per cent respectively in the community & comprehensive sector. A further point of comparison is the very high proportion of women not in any promotional post in the primary sector compared with the other sectors, 85.0 per cent in the primary sector compared with a low of 57.2 per cent in the community & comprehensive sector. The main cause of this difference is likely to be the system in operation before 1998 by which the age of pupils was a factor in calculating the number of promotional posts available in a school.

The figures presented in Table 4.1 show small increases since 1990 (Drudy and Lynch, 1993) in the proportion of women in B posts in all four sectors. Similarly, there are increases in the representation of women in A posts in the three second-level sectors. Three areas show a decrease in the representation of women, principalships in the primary and secondary sectors and vice-principalships in the secondary sector. The decrease in the primary sector is discussed in relation to the different types of principalships in the primary sector, below. The decreasing number of women in principalships in the secondary sector is considerable, from 50.5 per cent in 1991/92 (Drudy and Lynch, 1993) to the current figure of 42.8 per cent (Table 4.1). Two other factors are of some importance in considering this. First, the number of religious sisters has also decreased, from 81 per cent of principals in 1991/92 (Drudy and Lynch, 1993), to 66 per cent in 1996 (Lynch, 1997). Secondly, there is evidence from a survey of secondary schools that men are being appointed to principalships in single sex girls' secondary schools in 38 per cent of cases (ASTI, 1995). It is reasonable to conclude that these facts are linked. It is also evident that with the fall in the number of vocations to the religious life, that increasing numbers of lay teachers will be appointed to principalships. If the recent pattern of appointments continues, the proportion of women in principalships is likely to continue to decline in this sector.

The vocational sector shows the greatest change. There has been an increase in the proportion of women in all promoted positions in vocational schools since 1985 (Figure 4.1). In particular, there has been an increase of 140 per cent in the percentage of women principals, albeit from a very low base. Other posts show smaller but significant increases.

While the vocational sector shows an increase in the practice of promoting women teachers, the proportion of women who are promoted is still low relative to their overall representation in these schools. The only exception to this is the B posts where the ratio is somewhat higher.

FIGURE 4.1: WOMEN AS A PERCENTAGE OF TEACHERS IN PROMOTIONAL POSTS IN VOCATIONAL SCHOOLS, 1985/86 AND 1996

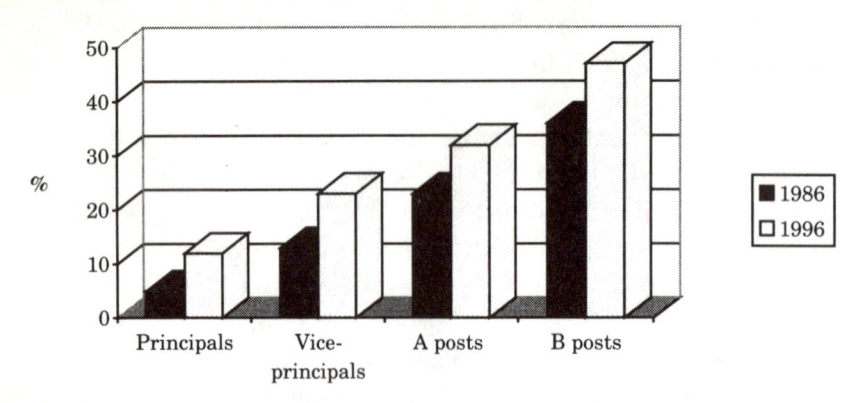

Sources: Vocational Education Committees and Drudy and Lynch (1993) for data related to 1985/86.

FACTORS AFFECTING RECENT CHANGES

In-depth analysis of recent changes in education can offer some insight into the processes in operation in the education system which are affecting the proportion of women in management positions. These include the decreasing role of women religious in principalships, discussed above. Three other factors are examined in this section: first, the process of rationalisation leading to amalgamation of schools, second, changes in the gender balance in types of principalships in the primary sector and finally, the relationship between age and promotion in all sectors.

The Process of Rationalisation and Amalgamations

International research reports school amalgamations and rationalisation as an important factor in the loss of women principals, in the Netherlands (Vermeulen and Ruijs, 1997) and the United Kingdom (Wilson, 1997a) (See chapter 2). There is evidence of a similar trend in the primary sector in this country. When a number of schools are amalgamated, the former principals who are not appointed to the position of principal in the newly amalgamated school retain the principal's allowance on a personal basis. Of those receiving this allowance on a personal basis in 1996, 82.6

per cent were women. While these figures are small, 3.8 per cent of the total number of principals, they show a trend in the effects of rationalisation on the proportion of women principals which is similar to that reported in other countries. At second level, there is no data available at present in relation to this question.

Types of Principalship and Gender in the Primary Sector

Previous research in this area has reported an increase over time in the proportion of women applying for and being appointed to principalships in the primary sector (Lynch, 1994). More detailed data giving the proportion of men and women teachers in different types of principalships has not been made available heretofore and is analysed here. There are four different types of principalships in Table 4.3.

- *Administrative principals*, also termed "walking principals". In schools with eight classroom teachers or more, the principal is not usually required to take personal responsibility for teaching a class group. The position is regarded as a full-time administrative post.

- *Teaching principals*. In schools with less than eight teachers, the principal has responsibility for a class group and may have some reduction in hours to allow for administrative work.

- *Acting administrative* and *acting teaching principals*.[4] Where the principal is on leave from school, either on a career break or on secondment to another post in education, the Board of Management appoints an acting principal in their place.

Table 4.3 presents a breakdown of the proportion of women in each of these types of principalships over a 20-year period.

---

[4] The proportion of "acting" principals is less than half of one per cent of all principals.

TABLE 4.3: TYPES OF PRIMARY PRINCIPALS BY GENDER, 1976, 1986 AND 1996

	1976	1986	1996
Types of Principals	Women as a %	Women as a %	Women as a %
Teaching	39.7	40.4	46.5
Administrative	51.5	46.9	45.1
Acting teaching	n/a	50	84.8
Acting administrative	n/a	n/a	85.7

Source: Department of Education and Science

In this breakdown of primary principals by type, a number of issues emerge. The pattern of appointments to administrative and teaching principalships has changed over the 20 year period represented in Table 4.2. In 1996, approximately 20 per cent of all principalships were administrative principalships. The balance of the proportion of women in the two types of principalships, administrative and teaching, has changed. The proportion of women holding teaching principalships has risen from 39.7 per cent in 1976 to 46.5 per cent in 1996, while simultaneously there has been a decrease in the proportion of women administrative principals from 51.5 per cent in 1976 to 45.1 per cent in 1996. While the percentage decrease is relatively small in the ten years to 1996, the figures show that the number of women in administrative principalships has fallen from 836 in 1986 to 672 in 1996, a drop of almost one-fifth. The extra workload involved in holding the position of principal at the same time as teaching full time may be seen as less attractive, but on the other hand the position involves continuing daily contact with students. It is in this position, rather than administrative principalships, that women are increasingly represented.

When a principal leaves the position on a temporary basis, the practice is generally for the vice-principal to be appointed to the position of principal in an acting capacity. The high proportion of women in vice-principalships is reflected in the proportion of women in acting positions. However, the number of acting principals is small and has a marginal impact on the overall picture.

A number of factors have been identified as having a negative impact on the proportion of women in principalships. These include the drop in the number of religious sisters who are principals, as outlined in Chapter 2, and the likelihood that men will be appointed to some of those positions. In the primary sector this is a less important issue than in the secondary sector, however, as just over ten per cent of women principals are religious sisters (Lynch, 1997). There is evidence that rationalisation and amalgamation of schools from single sex into coeducational institutions has led to a loss of women from principalships in the majority of cases. The third factor, hitherto undocumented but related to rationalisation, is the low levels of promotion of women to administrative principalships. It is evident from the figures in Table 4.3 that the increase in the appointment of women to principalships (Lynch, 1994) has been largely to teaching principal positions.

Age and Promotion: A Complex Relationship

Age is an important variable in considering the position of women teachers in the education system, not least because of the feminisation of the profession over time, detailed in Chapter 3. The high proportion of women among new entrants to teaching possibly exacerbates the imbalance in promotions. A breakdown of the incidence of promotion in the teaching body by age and gender which is presented in the following section will shed some light on this complex relationship.

Age and Promotion: The Primary Sector

The position of each age cohort of teachers in promotional posts in primary schools in Ireland in 1996 is presented in Table 4.4. This gives a picture of the career patterns of men and women in the primary sector and indicates what gender imbalances exist in the different age cohorts.

At first glance, the fact that 47.3. per cent of all principals are women (Table 4.1) could give an impression of gender balance. However, other figures in Table 4.4 indicate that this is not the case. First, the proportion of women and men who are principals from the total teaching body allows a clearer picture to emerge. While 38.7 per cent of men overall are principals, the proportion of women in this position is just ten per cent.

TABLE 4.4: PROMOTIONAL POSTS IN PRIMARY SCHOOLS, BY AGE COHORT AND GENDER, 1996

Posts	20-29		30-39		40-49		50-59		60+		Total	
	% Women	% Men	% Women	% Men	% Women	% Men	% Women	% Men	% Women	% Men	% Women	% Men
Principal	70.3	29.7	53.8	46.2	39.0	61.0	50.9	49.1	49.3	50.7	47.3	52.7
Vice-principal	86.7	13.3	91.4	8.6	77.2	22.8	84.8	15.2	88.3	11.7	82.9	17.1
A Post	n/a	n/a	69.2	30.8	62.7	37.3	71.4	28.6	91.7	8.3	68.0	32.0
B Post	37.5	63.5	77.1	22.9	73.3	26.7	79.9	20.1	88.3	11.7	76.2	23.8
No Post (% across)	85.5	15.5	84.8	15.2	81.2	18.8	91.7	8.3	91.4	8.6	85.0	15.0
No Post (% of age group)	96.9	92.5	85.3	69.1	61.3	35.0	48.5	14.2	46.0	14.1	71.8	44.3
Total %	84.9	15.1	81.8	18.2	71.2	28.8	76.5	23.5	76.8	23.2	77.7	22.3
Principals as % of age group	2.5	5.9	5.8	22.4	10.7	41.3	20.2	63.5	21.1	71.7	10.0	38.7

Source: Department of Education and Science.

A second significant figure is the percentage of women and men who have no promotional post. In the figures where the percentage is calculated in each group across, (percentage in all age groups), the percentage of teachers with no post who are women is always higher than the percentage of women in the cohort and the inverse is true for men. This increases to a high in the age groups 50 to 59 and over 60, where the proportion of teachers with no post who are women is over 90 per cent. When these figures are calculated as a percentage of the age group, i.e. percentages down, what emerges is that gender differences are evident in all age groups, even the age group 20 to 29. The gender gap increases up to the age group 50 to 59. Large differences exist between men and women in the age groups 40 to 49 and 50 to 59. In these age groups, the ratio of women to men who are not promoted is 3.4:1 and 3.3:1 respectively.

In relation to the percentages of men and women holding other promotional posts, the discussion regarding the position of vice-principal should be borne in mind. In addition, the total number of A posts is small in this sector, at less than 250 overall. Bearing these issues in mind, the very high proportion of women in vice-principal positions is notable, particularly in the age groups 30 to 39 where it is over 90 per cent.

The figures that give the clearest picture in Table 4.4 are possibly the percentage of principals in each age group, by gender. This gives an indication of the rate at which women and men achieve principalships throughout the age groups. In all age groups, men are considerably more likely to be in principalships than women. The ratio of men to women in principalships is more than 3:1 in all but the age group 20 to 29 and it rises to almost 4:1 in the age groups 30 to 39 and 40 to 49.

The age breakdown shows that women and men have very different career structures, with many women experiencing the "flat" career with no promotion described by Lortie (1975). This is, of course, not exclusive to teaching (O'Connor, 1999). It is notable that 46 per cent of the over 60 age group of women have not attained a promotion in their career. This compares with a corresponding figure of 14 per cent of men. Analysis of promotion patterns by age points to different career patterns for women and men. Specifically, a very high proportion of men have been promoted by the time they reach retirement age. Over 70 per cent of men over 60 years of age are principals, compared with just over 20 per cent of women. Table 4.4 also highlights the fact that the gender imbalances start in the youngest age groups and continue upwards. Analysis of these differences on a continuing basis over a period of time would better illuminate any changes that are taking place in the structure of women's and men's careers. The relationship, if any, between the promotion rates attained by men and women and the flow of teachers out of the profession remains a question that is beyond the scope of this study.

Age and Promotion: The Secondary Sector

In the secondary sector, the differences in promotion rates across age groups are considerably less than in the other second-level sectors (Table 4.1 above). The gender difference in relation to principalships has been discussed above. In the case of vice-principals, 40.9 per cent are women, considerably lower than the proportion of women in the teaching body in this sector (Table 4.1) and showing a decline from 43.1 per cent since 1990 (Drudy and Lynch, 1993). As the position of vice-principal has been appointed on the basis of seniority, as with A and B posts, the smaller representation of women raises questions. It is obviously beneficial to have the experience of vice-principal when applying for a principalship. In this regard, the lack of women vice-principals means fewer women are in an advantageous position in competition for principalships than would otherwise be the case. From a breakdown of vice-principals by age and gender an indication of a possible reason for this gender difference emerges (Table 4.5).

Men and women have been promoted to the position of vice-principal in proportion to their numbers except in the higher three age cohorts, 50-54, 55-59 and over 60. The women in these groups would generally have qualified and started their teaching career in the period prior to 1972, before equality legislation had been put in place, and are likely to have had to retire on marriage, or to have had breaks in career for family reasons. This is borne out by the proportion of these teachers on the top point of the salary scale (See Chapter 3). While 90.4 per cent of men over 50 years of age are on the top point of the salary scale, only 69.4 per cent of corresponding women are in this position. The implied interrupted career trajectories for women would have resulted in a loss of seniority in comparison with their male colleagues. This is likely to have contributed to the gender imbalance in the distribution of vice-principalships over the age of 50. Thus, while the system of promotion on the basis of seniority in the secondary sector has led to a relatively balanced proportion of men and women in A and B posts, it has not done so in the case of vice-principalships. This appears to be because of women's loss of seniority in schools due to interruptions in career. That is not to assume that women would have fared better in a system of open competition as clearly they have not done so in the other two second-level sectors.

TABLE 4.5: VICE-PRINCIPALSHIPS IN SECONDARY SCHOOLS BY AGE COHORT AND GENDER, 1996

Age Groups	30-34	35-39	40-44	45-49	50-54	55-59	60+	Total
Vice-principals: women	1	4	9	32	53	47	35	181
Vice-principals: men	0	1	8	31	83	87	52	262
% women in each age group	100.0	80.0	52.9	50.8	39.0	35.1	40.2	40.9
% men in each age group	0.0	20.0	47.1	49.2	61.0	64.9	59.8	59.1
Women as % of age cohort	0.1	0.3	0.7	3.1	8.8	11.8	18.3	2.4
Men as % of age cohort	0	0.1	0.8	2.9	10.6	21.9	26.0	4.9

Source: Department of Education and Science.

Age and Promotion: The Community & Comprehensive Sector

In community & comprehensive schools, promotion until recently has been on the basis of selection by an interview board without any union/management agreement on criteria for selection.[5] This

---

[5] In a small number of community & comprehensive schools, in-house agreements used seniority as the main criterion for promotion.

system has resulted in a gender imbalance in these schools in all promotional posts with the exception of B posts where the proportion of women is comparable with the proportion of women in the teaching body in the sector (Table 4.1). These promotion rates are therefore examined in depth here.

A breakdown of the promotional position of teachers by age cohort was sought and received from the Department of Education and Science and presented here (Table 4.6).[6] This table presents figures relating to gender, age and all promotional posts and in addition relating only to those holding A posts, vice-principalships and principalships. The lower part presents figures relating only to those holding A posts, vice-principalships and principalships. In general, the practice in these schools is for this group of senior teachers to form a middle management team who are active in decision-making and policy development in the school. It was considered important, therefore, to examine separately the gender balance in these senior posts.

From an initial examination of the figures in the top half of Table 4.6, it would appear that there is little variation in relation to promotion across age groups, irrespective of gender. While the exception here is the figure for men the age group 20 to 29, these findings should be interpreted with the caveat that the numbers are very small in this category. Taking the total figures into consideration, it is in the age group 40 to 49 that inequalities emerge. It was clear from Table 4.1, however, that women tended to be concentrated in the B post positions and that much greater inequalities are evident in the higher promotional posts. The lower part of Table 4.6 gives the figures for promotions to upper and middle management positions, principalships, vice-principalships and A posts.

The lack of representation of women in these management and middle management promotional posts is evident, with the exception of the age group 20–29. In terms of the overall figures, women form just over 30 per cent of this group, men, just under 70 per

---

[6] The total figures used here are slightly different to those in Table 4.1 above, as the Department of Education and Science figures include those holding posts on a personal entitlement basis and because one school is missing from Table 4.1.

cent. The proportion of all women and men who hold these positions, the proportion of men is twice that of women, 32.5 per cent and 14.5 per cent respectively.

TABLE 4.6: TEACHERS IN ALL PROMOTED POSTS AND IN SENIOR POSITIONS (PRINCIPALSHIPS, VICE-PRINCIPALSHIPS AND A POSTS) IN COMMUNITY & COMPREHENSIVE SCHOOLS BY GENDER AND AGE GROUP, 1996

Age Groups	20-29	30-39	40-49	50-59	60+	Totals
% in all promotional posts: women	68.2	53.6	43.6	27.7	28.8	41.9
% in all promotional posts: men	31.8	46.4	56.4	62.3	71.2	58.9
Women in promotional posts as % of total age cohort	6.1	40.2	73.0	61.2	48.6	48.0
Men in promotional posts as % of total age cohort	50.0	39.3	73.3	81.9	70.0	64.5
% in principalships, vice-principalships and A posts who are women	100.0	50.6	32.7	20.6	25.5	30.2
% in principalships, vice-principalships and A posts who are men	0.0	49.4	67.3	79.4	74.5	69.8
Women in senior promotional posts as % of total age cohort	0.4	7.8	22.8	27.0	37.1	14.5
Men in senior promotional posts as % of total age cohort	0.0	8.6	36.3	53.2	63.3	32.5

Source: Department of Education and Science.

Those under 30 years of age show a higher rate of promotions for women but the proportion of men in this group is a very small minority (n=14) as discussed in Chapter 3. Gender differences emerge in the senior positions in the age group 40 to 49 and increase in the higher age groups. In the age group 40 to 49, 22.8 per cent of women have been promoted to these senior posts, compared with 36.3 per cent of men, a ratio of 1.6:1. In the age group 50 to 59 this ratio increases to 2.0:1 and in the over 60 age group it is 1.7:1. A number of gender differences in relation to the career trajectories of men and women in this sector have been discussed in Chapter 3. These differences include the more interrupted career trajectories of women, and the fact that men tend to enter teaching later than women in this sector. The impact of these two factors would affect the relative seniority of men and women in the sector. Seniority has not been a criteria for promotion in this sector. It should be noted, however, that an unquantifiable issue is the influence of amalgamations of secondary schools into this sector, where previous appointments on the basis of seniority would be carried over by teachers into the new school situation. The large differences in promotion rates for men and women may be the result of other unidentified factors. As the teachers in senior positions in many of the schools and colleges of this sector are those who formulate policy for the school, then women have very little voice in the management structures of these schools.

Age and Promotion: The Vocational Sector

As in the community & comprehensive sector, promotion in this sector has been on the basis of selection on open competition rather than seniority and a gender imbalance in all promotional posts with the exception of B posts has developed (Table 4.1). The same method of presentation and analysis of data is used to examine this in depth. Because of the changing gender balance of the teaching body in this sector, the most illuminating figures are those that indicate what proportion of women and men in any age cohort have attained promotion.

Given that promotion in the vocational sector has been based on open competition, the difference in the loss of career time for women outlined in Chapter 3 should not lead to significant loss of promotion for women. Yet the pattern of inequality is clear from the age group 30 to 39 upwards, with the greatest imbalance in the age group 40 to 49. The ratio of men and women in promotional posts in that age group is 2.1:1. In Chapter 3, it emerged that there is little difference in career trajectories of women and men in this age group: it is in the older age groups that women tend to have lost career time. The expectation would be that the effect of interruptions in women's careers would not seriously impede promotion prospects for this group, yet it is the group with the least favourable position in relation to promotion.

TABLE 4.7: TEACHERS IN ALL PROMOTED POSTS AND IN SENIOR POSITIONS (PRINCIPALSHIPS, VICE-PRINCIPALSHIPS AND A POSTS) IN THE VOCATIONAL SECTOR BY GENDER AND AGE GROUP, 1996

Age Groups	20-29	30-39	40-49	50-59	60+	Totals
% in all promotional posts: women	73.0	66.0	45.1	21.4	25.0	38.1
% in all promotional posts: men	27.0	34.0	54.9	78.6	75.0	61.9
Women in promotional posts as % of total age cohort	17.2	46.7	52.1	60.3	70.0	45.9
Men in promotional posts as % of total age cohort	19.1	55.9	79.7	85.6	87.5	74.2
% women in principalships, vice-principalships and A posts	60.0	55.6	28.3	17.3	19.1	27.1
% men in principalships, vice-principalships and A posts	40.0	44.4	71.7	82.7	80.9	72.9
Women in senior promotional posts as % of total age cohort	0.7	10.2	19.9	29.8	36.7	14.9
Men in senior promotional posts as % of total age cohort	1.4	15.8	41.4	55.3	64.6	39.8

Source: Vocational Education Committees. One Vocational Education Committee Area missing.

Significant imbalances in promotion rates to senior positions by gender are evident in the second part of Table 4.7. A comparison by age cohort indicates that this trend does not vary by age but exists throughout the system. Excluding the age group 20 to 29 where figures are very small, the ratio of promoted men to women is approaching 2:1 in all but the age cohort 30 to 39, where it is 1.5:1. Again, it is the age group 40 to 49 that shows the greatest imbalance, with a ratio of 2.1:1.

As in the case of the community & comprehensive sector, if this group of senior teachers acts as a senior management team as is the usual practice, women will have little influence in the decision-making areas of education in this sector.

APPLICATIONS AND APPOINTMENTS TO PROMOTIONAL POSITIONS

The issue of the rate of application for promotion by women teachers has been highlighted as an explanation for the lack of women in senior positions in education. The findings in this area are presented in detail in relation to three sectors in which data is available, namely the primary, community & comprehensive and vocational sectors. It was not possible to gather data on the secondary sector for this study, but the indications are that the rate of application for principalships on the part of women is lowest in this sector overall (Lynch, 1997; Warren, 1997).

Applications and Appointments: The Primary Sector

Since 1988 at primary level, appointments of women to principalships have been more than 50 per cent of the total each year. Since 1989, women have formed the majority of applicants for principalships overall (Warren, 1997). However, this is far short of the proportion of women teachers in this sector as a whole (77.7 per cent). Table 4.8 shows a breakdown of applications for principalship and newly appointed principals by gender in three two-year intervals over a period of 10 years. The proportion of women applicants has risen steadily and the proportion of women appointed to principalships has been consistently higher than the percentage of women applicants.

This pattern of women teachers achieving a higher percentage of appointments in proportion to their applications has been evident in the process for some years (Lynch, 1997). Between 1986 and 1996, the proportion of women principals has risen from 42.0

per cent in 1986 to 47.3 per cent in 1996 (Table 4.1), a gain of just over 5 per cent in ten years.

TABLE 4.8: APPLICANTS AND NEWLY APPOINTED PRINCIPALS IN PRIMARY SCHOOLS BY GENDER OVER THREE SEPARATE PERIODS OF TWO YEARS

	Applicants		Appointments	
	Women	Men	Women	Men
1985-87	397	838	80	105
As a %	32.2%	67.8%	43.2%	56.8%
1989-91	692	698	106	67
As a %	49.8%	50.2%	61.3%	38.7%
1994-96	772	728	167	125
As a %	51.5%	48.5%	57.2%	42.8%

Source: Lynch (1997) and INTO Annual Reports.

While both the rate of application and rate of appointment of women to principal have increased steadily over the years, questions remain about the gender balance in the various categories of principalship. In relation to the position of administrative principal, there has been a considerable decrease in the proportion of women since 1986. No data is available on the rate of application for or appointment to the different categories of principalship.

Applications and Appointments: The Community & Comprehensive Sector

In the community & comprehensive sector, data relating to vice-principals, A posts and B posts was collected.[7] Table 4.9 gives the national figures on applications and promotions as returned by the relevant schools. The "success rate" in Table 4.9 refers to the number of successful applicants as a percentage of the total number of applicants by gender.

---

[7] Four schools are omitted as data was not received in one case while the appointments in the relevant period were based on seniority in three other schools.

TABLE 4.9 PERCENTAGES OF APPLICATIONS AND APPOINTMENTS TO POSTS OF RESPONSIBILITY IN COMMUNITY & COMPREHENSIVE SCHOOLS, BY GENDER, 1993-96

	Vice-principal			A Post			B Post		
	Women %	Men %	Total (N)	Women %	Men %	Total (N)	Women %	Men %	Total (N)
Applications	42.8	57.2	201	47.0	53.0	489	53.8	46.2	672
Appointments	34.8	65.2	23	51.4	48.6	105	59.6	40.4	255
Success Rate*	9.3	13.0	11.4	23.5	19.7	21.5	41.9	33.0	37.9

Source: Community & comprehensive schools. Four schools omitted.

* Success rate: successful candidates as a percentage of applicants in each column.

Over 40 per cent of applicants for vice-principalships in the period 1993 to 1996 are women, as presented in Table 4.9. This is almost double the rate of applications to these positions reported for the period 1992 to 1994, which was 22.8 per cent (O'Hara, 1994). Appointments of women have also risen, but remain at a lower rate, 34.8 per cent of the total number of appointments. The success rate of men in applying for vice-principalships is considerably higher than that of women in this sector.

The rate of applications from women is higher for the lower promotional posts. For the positions of A post, it is 47 per cent of the total, while in the case of B posts, it is higher again at almost 54 per cent. The success rate for women for these positions is higher than that of men, in contrast with the situation in relation to vice-principalships. In the case of B posts, their success rate is 27 per cent higher than that of men.

While the proportion of women applying for vice-principalships has increased since the early 90's, their rate of success has been considerably below that of male applicants. Women teachers now form almost 50 per cent of applicants for A posts and more than 50 per cent of applicants for B posts in this sector. Considering the proportion of women in the sector who do not hold promotional posts, (57.2 per cent, Table 4.1) the rate of application by women is below that by men for all posts including the position of B post.

Applications and Appointments: The Vocational Sector

In the vocational sector, data relating to applications and appointments for principalships, vice-principalships, A posts and B posts was collected for the period 1993-96. However, two of the largest Vocational Education Committee areas had no record of applications and hence were excluded from this section. One other Vocational Education Committee area provided no data. The effect that these three missing areas might have on the figures cannot be estimated and the findings in Tables 4.10 and 4.11 should be interpreted with this caveat in mind.

In the data presented in Table 4.10, the rate at which women apply for principalships is just over 20 per cent and for vice-principalships it is over 30 per cent. The main finding is that women teachers are not applying for these positions at the same rate as men. It is notable that the rate of appointment is generally in direct proportion to the rate of application of women. Thus, the success rate of women applicants is equal to or better than that of men for these positions. As in the community & comprehensive sector, in relation to A and B posts, the rate of application from women increases as the post level decreases. In the case of A posts, the success rate of women is slightly better than that of men, while in the case of B posts, women are considerably more successful than men, with a success rate 28.8 per cent higher than that of men.

On initial examination it would appear that women are applying for A and B posts at the same rate as men in this sector, but a greater number and proportion of women teachers are without posts and are therefore eligible for posts. Table 4.11 examines the application rates of men and women in relation to the total number of "eligible teachers" for vice-principalship and A and B posts.

While almost all teachers are eligible to apply for A posts and vice-principalships, in practice teachers need some administrative experience in order to have a realistic chance of promotion. For the purposes of this research, the pool of eligible teachers for vice-principalships has therefore been confined to A post holders and similarly the pool of eligible teachers for A posts has been confined to B post holders, for comparison purposes. The data in this table cannot take account of repeat applications or applications for positions which are two or more levels above the current position of the teacher. Therefore, the available data can only be used as an indication of a trend.

Women apply in the same proportions as men for A posts but not for the other two positions. Considering the imbalance in the teaching body in this sector, this needs to be addressed by the authorities in these organisations. Because of the gender imbalance in postholders overall, a greater number of women hold no post and are eligible for a B post, yet this is the area which shows the greatest imbalance. The ratio of applications as a percentage of the eligible group of men and women is 1.6:1. A variety of reasons have been suggested why women do not apply for management positions, such as loss of contact with students and the recognised heavy work-load involved in performing the role of a principal or vice-principal. However, in relation to B posts, it is difficult to suggest a reason why women do not apply. This would appear to be an

TABLE 4.10: APPLICATIONS AND APPOINTMENTS FOR POSTS OF RESPONSIBILITY IN THE VOCATIONAL SECTOR, BY GENDER, 1993-96

	Principal			Vice-principal			A Post			B Post		
	Women %	Men %	Total (N)	Women %	Men %	Total (N)	Women %	Men %	Total (N)	Women %	Men %	N
Applications	20.8	79.2	154	31.5	68.5	387	48.7	51.3	791	57.1	42.9	813
Appointments	23.8	76.2	21	31.1	68.9	45	48.9	51.1	180	63.2	36.8	391
Success Rate*	15.6	13.1	13.6	11.5	11.7	11.6	22.9	22.7	22.8	53.2	41.3	48.1

Source: Vocational Education Committees Three Vocational Educational Committee are missing.

* Success rate: successful candidates as a percentage of applicants in each column.

TABLE 4.11: APPLICATION RATES FOR POSTS OF RESPONSIBILITY IN VOCATIONAL SCHOOLS, AS A PERCENTAGE OF THE NUMBER OF ELIGIBLE TEACHERS, BY GENDER, 1993-96

	Vice-principal		A Post		B Post	
	Women	Men	Women	Men	Women	Men
Number eligible	1136	1574	825	916	1434	687
Applications as % of eligible group	10.7	16.8	46.7	44.3	32.4	50.8

Three VEC areas not included. "Eligible" teachers calculated as the number of teachers in the next position down.

area where further research would prove beneficial in the process of understanding the patterns of inequality evident in these schools.

SUMMARY

While women appear to fare relatively well in the primary sector, the evidence shows that women and men have very different careers within that sector, with almost half of women not achieving any promotion. The experience of women in the secondary sector in relation to promotion has also been relatively successful, but the fall in the proportion of women principals is an important indication of changes taking place in this sector. The lack of information relating to the processes involved in that change is regrettable.

When promotion has been on open competition in the community & comprehensive and vocational sectors, the result has been a low representation of women. While there has been an increase in the proportion of women in principalships and vice-principalships in these sectors, this is in comparison with a very low starting point.

The findings in relation to promotion and gender in each sector are summarised here.

Summary: The Primary Sector

A number of issues have been examined in relation to gender and promotion in the primary sector. These include the current situation in relation to the proportion of women in principalships, the effects of rationalisation and amalgamations, the question of promotion of men and women to different types of principalship, the relationship between age and promotion and the question of the rate of application for principalship from women.

- Almost 40 per cent of men who are primary teachers are principals, compared with ten per cent of women.

- It can be deduced, from the high proportion of women in the group of teachers in receipt of a principal's allowance on a personal basis, that as primary schools are amalgamated, women who are principals lose their position in considerably greater numbers than men

- An analysis of the proportion of women in the different types of principalships at primary level, administrative and teaching principalships, indicates that the proportion of women administrative principals has fallen consistently since 1976, from 52 per cent to 45 per cent. This has not been evident here-to-fore as overall figures only were available. Thus the small increase in the proportion of women in principalships in the primary sector (from 42 per cent up to 47 per cent in 20 years), has been due to a growth in the proportion of women in the position of teaching principal and the position of acting principal. The number of women in administrative principalships has dropped by a fifth since 1986.

- Seventy-two per cent of men in the over 60 age group are promoted to a principalship, compared with 21 per cent of women. So, women, not men, have a flat career in teaching. In fact, only 14 per cent of men in that age group did not hold a promotional post, compared with 46 per cent of women.

- While women comprise over 50 per cent of applicants for principalships in recent years, this is well below the rate of application of men. However, women applicants have had more success than men who applied. No information is available on the rate of application and appointment of men and women to the different types of principalships.

Summary: The Secondary Sector

While there is a balance in the proportion of men and women in promotional posts in this sector, there is evidence of change in the area of principalships. Data in relation to this issue is limited. However, some trends are evident in this area and in relation to the relatively low proportion of women in the position of vice-principal.

- The overall proportion of women in principalships at 42.8 per cent masks considerable variation by school type and variation in the percentage of women principals who are religious sisters.

- It is evident that the decrease in the proportion of women in principalships has coincided with a decline in the number of religious sisters in these positions. This is likely to continue unless action is taken to reverse this trend.
- Since 1990, the proportion of women in vice-principalships shows a decline from 43.1 per cent to the more recent figure of 40.9 per cent.
- In this sector, just over 40 per cent of vice-principals are women, compared with 58 per cent of the total teaching body. Analysis shows that an imbalance emerges in the age groups over 50. From a comparison of age with point on the salary scale, evidence of loss of career time on the part of women indicated that this may be a reason for this imbalance. Women in the age group over 50 appear to have lost career time and hence, have lost seniority in this sector with the resulting imbalance in the position of vice-principal.

Summary: The Community & Comprehensive Sector

A number of issues are examined in this chapter in relation to promotion and gender in this sector. These include the overall gender imbalance, development of inequalities in relation to age, the position of women in the senior or middle management and management positions (principal, vice-principal and A post), and the rate of application and appointment of women and men to the positions of vice-principal, A post and B post. The impact of school amalgamation and the carry-over of posts of responsibility previously appointed is unknown.

- Despite recent small increases, women are under-represented in this sector in all promotional posts except that of B post. In the case of principalships, the proportion is the lowest of any sector, at ten per cent.
- In the key positions from which a middle management team is usually drawn in these schools, A post, vice-principal and principal, the proportions are much less favourable to women,

with over 30 per cent of men in one of these positions compared with 15 per cent of women.

- An analysis of promotion by age and gender reveals that inequalities emerge in the age group 40 to 49 upwards in relation to promotion to senior positions, with the greatest inequality in the age group 50 to 59.

- The rate of applications from women for vice-principalships has almost doubled in recent years, from 22.8 per cent to 40.8 per cent (1993-96). However, the success rate of men who applied is 40 per cent higher than that of women. In the case of A and B posts of responsibility, women form about half of applicants and have a higher success rate than men in the case of both types of posts. Despite their success rate, it is evident that relative to their overall representation, women are not applying at the same rate as men for vice-principalships or for B posts in this sector.

Summary: The Vocational Sector

Issues that have emerged in this sector are similar to those in the community & comprehensive sector. These include the gender imbalance in the current situation, recent changes in these figures, the relationship between age and promotion and rates of application and promotion for all promotional posts in this sector over the period 1993 to 1996.

- The proportion of women in promotional posts overall in the vocational sector is 46 per cent compared with 74 per cent of men. In the senior promotional posts of principal, vice-principal and A post, the proportions are much less favourable to women, with 15 per cent of women in one of these positions compared with 40 per cent of men.

- There has been an increase in the proportion of women in all promoted positions in the vocational sector since 1985. The greatest growth has been in the position of principal where there has been an increase of 140 per cent in the proportion of women principals, albeit from a very low starting point.

- The inequalities in this sector are more pronounced for the age groups over 50, but the gender imbalance is evident for all age groups. In all age groups over 30, there is a higher proportion of men in promotional posts compared with women. In relation to the senior posts of principal, vice-principal and A post, the trend does not vary by age but exists throughout the system. The chance of a man being promoted to one of these positions is almost twice that of a woman in this sector in all age groups over 30.

- Just over 20 per cent of applicants for principalships in this sector are women and their success rate is slightly higher than that of men. This is a major change from 1985 when only five per cent of all principals in this sector were women.

- Applications from and appointments of women to vice-principalships in the vocational sector also show major changes, with almost a third of these positions going to women. This remains less than the proportion of applicants from women in the community & comprehensive sector for this position.

- Women form almost half of the applicants for A posts and their success rate is equal to that of the male applicants for these posts. In the case of B posts, women form 57 per cent of applicants and have a higher success rate than men.

- While the rate of application from women for A posts was on a par with that of men, women had a much lower rate of application for B posts relative to their eligibility (32.4 per cent and 50.8 per cent respectively).

The above findings outline the recent trends and developments with regard to the participation of women in managerial posts across the education system. An issue that cannot be clarified by using figures and statistics alone is why women are not applying for promotion to principalships or to lower grade posts, considering that they form the majority of teachers in the system. In the following chapter, this and related issues are fully explored.

Chapter 5

WOMEN IN EDUCATIONAL MANAGEMENT: PERCEPTIONS AND BARRIERS

INTRODUCTION

This study has highlighted the situation in education in Ireland, that increasingly women are the majority of teachers at primary and second level, but that in the field of management in schools they are poorly represented. The analysis in this chapter goes beyond the central issue of why women do not apply for principalships, to ask other more probing questions:

- Are there structural barriers in the system of promotions that discourage women from applying for promotion?

- Are there aspects of the Irish educational system that discourage women from applying for promotion, particularly in the secondary sector?

- What are women's perceptions of management and what is the impact of those perceptions?

- What impact does the pattern of power relations have on the attitudes of women to promotion in education?

These questions are now explored using a qualitative method of open interviews and focus group discussion (Appendix 3).

SOURCES

In order to explore the issues raised by the data presented in Chapters 3 and 4, a number of interviews were held with women teachers from the four sectors and with persons involved in policy development in education and with management of schools. The interviews were based on open-ended questions so as to allow issues to emerge for the individuals involved. The interviewees held a variety of promotional posts, vice-principalships, A and B Posts and some had no posts. A total of eight persons were interviewed. In addition to discussions with individual teachers, a focus group was organised to explore the issues that had arisen in relation to women in secondary schools, particularly the underlying reasons why so few women from these schools apply for principalships (Appendix 3).

A focus group is defined as a small group of people who meet with a trained researcher or facilitator to discuss selected topics in a non-threatening environment. The group explores perceptions, attitudes, feelings and ideas and group interactions are utilised in the discussion (Wilson, 1997). While the opinions and perceptions expressed in these discussions cannot be taken as representative of any specific group, what emerged, along with the data presented in Chapters 3 and 4 and indications from the research literature in Chapter 2, gave an indication of important issues and areas for further exploration in relation to women and management positions in education. Focus groups are increasingly being used in research and proved a very useful source in this instance.

Evidence from equality cases taken under the 1977 Employment Equality Act has also been examined as a source of information regarding possible career blocks for women in education. Issues emerging from the interviews, the focus group and the equality cases are woven together in order to attempt to give insights into the questions posed at the beginning of the chapter.

STRUCTURAL BARRIERS TO WOMEN IN MANAGEMENT

In discussing this issue, Shakeshaft (1989) has identified different stages at which barriers may arise that block the career progress of women more than men. A certain proportion of possible applicants are filtered out of the process at each stage, hence the term "filters" has been used in the analysis of the process (Shakeshaft, 1989; Lynch, 1993). In this study, the four stages in appointments to principalships are referred to as "filters". The first step of getting an opportunity to apply for a position as it becomes vacant is the first filter. The next filter is the stage of shortlisting for interview. The third filter is the interview itself and the processes involved in it. The final filter is the selection of the successful candidate. The perceptions of women in relation to these structures, as ascertained in interviews and focus group discussions, are reported here along with evidence from reported equality cases.

The First Filter: The Application

The process of application for principalships in Ireland is required to be by open competition in schools in which salaries are paid by the Department of Education and Science. Two specific issues were identified as creating barriers at this stage. One of the primary teachers interviewed for this study stated that she felt she would not be considered a strong candidate if she did not ask the chairperson of her Board of Management for a reference when applying for a principalship. As she perceived that he did not approve of women principals, she felt that any reference from him would be of little value. As a teacher in a rural area who, for family reasons, could not move a long distance for a teaching position or a position of principal, she felt that her career was blocked by this circumstance.

A second issue which arose in relation to the application stage is the type of application form for principalship now commonly used in secondary schools. The detailed questions in this form relating to one's approach to education on a wide variety of issues require a considerable amount of time to answer. An interviewee involved in selecting principals suggested that it is in fact acting as a filter as the requests for the application form for principalships in secondary schools are very much greater in number than the applications finally received. It was this person's perception that the form may filter out women more than men as the rate of applications from women has been very low in these instances.

The Second Filter: Shortlisting

In making decisions about criteria for shortlisting, selection committees may inadvertently reduce the pool of women who may apply for a position. For instance, because of the low proportion of women in middle management positions in the community & comprehensive and vocational sector and the low proportion of women in vice-principalships in the secondary sector (Chapter 4), a decision to shortlist only those with a certain level of experience will in effect create a structural barrier for women more than for men. While this would operate particularly at the level of appointing a principal, it also occurs at other levels.

An example of such a barrier in action occurred in 1993. In that year, a selection committee in a school took the decision to interview only those who held an A post when a vacancy for a vice-principalship was being filled, thereby blocking a number of female internal and external candidates (Equality Officer Report No. 1/1994). The decision ignored the context of how, in certain sectors such as the community & comprehensive and vocational sectors, women are under-represented in promotional posts that the selection committee deemed necessary for shortlisting. To what extent such decisions are made in selection procedures for principalships remains unknown as there is little information in the public domain regarding this issue. The procedural decisions made by selection committees remain confidential to those committees unless the decision is challenged by a person taking action in the form of an Equality Case under the 1977 Equality Act or some other legal challenge.

The Third Filter: The Interview

An issue that emerged in discussion with interviewees, was that selection committees can be composed only of men or of a very high proportion of men. Whether or not the interviews held by such committees are fair, the impact for the women who experienced them was clear. They reported feeling dismayed and thrown off balance by the experience. While no men were interviewed in connection with this practice, it would not be unreasonable to suggest that men would not be discomfited in the same way and would be at an advantage compared with women in the stressful situation of a formal interview. No matter how fair an interview such a committee could conduct, the outcome is influenced by the negative effect of the composition of the selection committee on some women applicants, and perhaps a positive effect for some men.

At primary level, there is a requirement for men and women to be represented on the selection committee. In September 1997 a circular issued from the Department of Education and Science to the Chief Executive Officers of all Vocational Education Committees instructed these bodies that in future appointments to all promotional positions, there must be "appropriate gender balance" on the selection committee (Circular 29/97). In the absence of any guidelines for good practice in selection procedures, the effectiveness of this recommendation remains a question for future research.

In discussion with an interviewee who has been involved in the appointment of a number of principals and other promotional posts, the comment was made that on occasion women appeared not to have fully thought through the implications of their appointment to the position in question. In fact, the interviewee reported that a number of women who had applied for principalships had expressed the belief that they would not be appointed to the position they sought. Furthermore, it was the perception of the interviewee that this affected the performance of the candidate at interview as they had failed fully to think through the consequences of a successful application and were not, in fact, prepared for success.

The Fourth Filter: The Appointment

The basis on which the appointment of a principal, vice-principal or post holder is made has been very vague in the past, with each selection committee agreeing its own criteria. A recent agreement on appointments to posts of responsibility (ASTI, 1997) sets out criteria on which candidates are awarded points at interview. At the level of appointments to principalships, however, the process remains dependent on the efforts of each selection committee and remains confidential.

Summary: The Four Filters

There is a danger that women will find their career blocked at each filter point in the process as outlined above:

- When they need a reference from a person in a position of authority who has a biased attitude (real or perceived) towards women in management

- By the use of an elaborate application form, which may or may not be useful or necessary

- By the decisions of selection committees which filter out teachers who have not held a certain grade of promotion, irrespective of levels of administrative experience or ability

- By women's own lack of preparedness for success, and finally

- By the predominance of men on selection committees.

EFFECTS OF THE IRISH EDUCATIONAL SYSTEM

This section addresses the second question, set out at the beginning of this chapter, regarding what particular aspects of the Irish educational system may discourage women from applying for promotion. As the level of application for principalship from women is very low in the secondary sector (Chapter 4), this question was explored only in relation to that sector. Discussions with individual teachers and managers and analysis of the focus group discussions pinpointed the importance of attitudes in forming barriers to women's careers in education. In a number of single sex girls' schools represented in the focus group, only one woman had applied for the position of principal from the staff when it became vacant and in the case of one school, no woman had applied. In that instance, the staff of more than 40 teachers was over 90 per cent female and a male principal was appointed from outside the school. A number of issues that are unique to the Irish situation arose in the discussion at this point in the focus group and are discussed below.

Attitudes of Women to Applications for Principalship

In situations where seniority has been a central criterion for promotion, women have progressed in promotional positions (Table 4.1). From the focus group discussion it emerged that this situation also appears to have led to particular perceptions and attitudes in relation to seeking promotion in secondary schools. The same dynamic may or may not occur in primary schools but this was not investigated in the case of this study. The problem of putting oneself forward as being above one's peers goes against the socialisation of women (Case, 1994) and is seen as damaging to relationships in schools. An interviewee working in the area of policy development in education voiced the opinion that where teachers are working well as a team in a school and there has been no tradition of competition for promotion, women then do not wish to step out of the group and put themselves forward as a possible leader. The question of what effect such a move would have on relationships in the team would be a concern, whether or not the woman was a successful candidate. The importance of a feeling of connection and good working relationships were identified as central, and their possible loss a potential block for some women (Boulton and Coldron, 1998). The socialisation process which girls experience has been identified as encouraging girls into a system of co-operation with peers which appears to remain a strong force in later life (Case, 1994). A related barrier was identified in the focus group in relation to this.

One participant who had worked in another career highlighted the effect:

> "Another reason why women are very slow is that we have no history of promotion. I worked in a public body and you were in an atmosphere, even at junior level, of "oh, this . . . (promotion) . . . is coming up . . ." there was a sort of a cult of promotion. (In teaching) it was pointless aspiration really and . . . maybe the younger people won't feel that. . . ."

While the major effect of the seniority agreement has been to secure promotion for women, it has meant that those women in primary and secondary schools are not accustomed to competing for promotion. The only time they have to decide whether or not to actively seek promotion is when the principalship is advertised. The hesitancy in women seeking promotion identified in the literature (Gold, 1996) is intensified under these conditions.

Religious Sisters as Role Models

The fact that a section of Irish schools have been managed by women over a long period has provided women teachers and students with female role models in powerful, influential positions. What positive impact this may have had is an unknown. In the secondary sector, the figures relating to the proportion of women applying for principalships in single sex girls' schools are not available apart from data gathered for the period 1986 to 1989. In those figures, women applied in relatively high proportions, composing 40 per cent of applicants in girls' schools (ASTI, 1996), but the response rate to the surveys was very low, at 30.1 per cent. What emerged from the focus group was, that in a number of single sex girls' schools, there were few or no applications from women from within the school. One trustee body, the Conference of the Religious of Ireland, has expressed concern at the low proportion of women applying for principalships in the secondary sector and has taken some steps to remedy the situation (CORI, 1994).

In individual interviews and the focus group discussions it became clear that some of the religious sisters who were principals modelled a level of commitment of time and energy to the job that other women felt they could not match. This arose in different parts of the focus group discussion and from a number of participants. In relation to a principal who was a religious sister, one participant said:

> "(we) . . . left it up to her. . . she worked long hours . . . you used to think of it as a job that a lay person couldn't do . . . maybe it was projected that way. . ."

Another participant concurred:

> "We saw the principalship as a nun's (religious sister's) job when we were in our thirties . . . we just didn't think . . . I saw the principal as somebody way up there. . . . It never dawned on me that in five or ten years' time that I could go that way . . ."

Another woman identified the lack of opportunities as a factor that stifled ambition:

> "When I went into teaching the principals were invariably religious so it didn't matter how ambitious you were . . . unless you left teaching and went into another area it was pointless ambition really . . ."

An interviewee in the area of management suggested that the lack of delegation in these school had a particular impact on middle management, i.e. A and B post holders. It was the perception of this interviewee that in many secondary schools, teachers had little experience of meaningful middle management positions and thus had not had an opportunity to develop their leadership abilities. This argument would also hold, however, for men in secondary schools and does not explain the very low proportion of women applying for principalships in these schools, overall less than ten per cent. This suggests that the reasons for the reluctance of women in the secondary sector to apply for a position as principal are more complex than a simple response to the perceived demands of the job and must be viewed in the context of women's position in the workforce as a whole.

The question posed in this section was in relation to the particular aspects of the Irish education system that appear to create barriers for women. The issues highlighted here were perceived as barriers. The negative impact of women's perceptions of the work involved in a principalship appears to have contributed, at times, to the very low level of applications from women for the principalships of secondary schools.

WOMEN'S PERCEPTION OF MANAGEMENT

A number of issues arose in the focus group and individual discussions that highlighted the negative perceptions of women regarding the position of principal. Three aspects are examined here: women's attitude to career, perceptions of the position of principal and the inherent lack of support in the system and finally, style of management and its impact.

Women's Attitude to Career

The issue of the extra caring work done by women was identified as a crucial point in discouraging women from seeking the position of principal. One participant of the focus group highlighted this and there was general agreement from the other participants with her statement:

> "Most women still feel responsible for the family at home and there is this job that takes up so much extra time . . ."

The issue of feeling responsible for the family home was also highlighted by another participant who felt that she could not shake off the feelings that had been instilled into her as a child:

> "You come home late after working hard and maybe no one has done any cleaning or tidying for days and the house is in a mess . . . and then somebody calls and you feel so guilty and ashamed . . ."

There was recognition in the group that even where women are earning as much as their partners, or more, the housework is seen as their responsibility and women feel that their social standing is judged by the level of tidiness of their home. While there was a recognition that this judgement may be very much in their own minds, it was shared by many of the women in the group. One interviewee referred to the same issue from another point of view. She explained that if she were to become principal of a school she would need to employ others to fulfil aspects of the roles that she normally sees to in the home. The extra payment for the position of principal would, she believed, disappear on paying for the necessary support structures in the home.

More importantly, perhaps, was a recognition in the focus group and from one individual interviewee that it is essential to give time to the care of children and teenagers and that a job that would mean getting home late in the evening would cut into that time too much. There was a consensus in the focus group that women will only apply for time-consuming positions when their children have reached a stage where they are more independent. This point also came across strongly in research on the women principals in secondary schools in Ireland (Mullarkey, 1994).

Perceptions of the Position of Principal and Lack of Support

The issue of the demands of the job of principal and the lack of support for a principal in secondary schools was identified as an important factor. One member of the focus group put the case succinctly when she stated:

> "I wouldn't dream of applying for a principalship . . . it would take up so much of my personal time. I have other interests outside school. . . . I am not interested in having a telephone call on Christmas Eve to tell me the pipes are burst . . ."

An interviewee who was a primary teacher also explained that many teachers regard the position of a teaching principal as a most unattractive one, again because of the lack of support structures for principals and because of the impossibility of doing two jobs well: taking responsibility for teaching a group of students, and being principal of the school. O'Connor (1998) and others have suggested that predominantly female professions have had difficulties accessing adequate resources, leading to a coping style of management which puts extra pressure on middle and senior managers. The issue of lack of support structures was raised in the focus group discussion and in interviews as a distinct barrier for women considering applying for a principalship.

The focus group participants felt that because of women's values in relation to caring for family and quality of life, women consider the negative aspects of the job and many decide that it is not worth the extra work involved. One interviewee who holds a vice-principalship and who is in a two-person, two-career situation, highlighted this:

> "I don't feel *driven* to get promotion at all costs, I am taking other things into account — my family, my quality of life, the lack of support structures in schools, the isolation of the job. . . . I have other priorities and interests where I get a lot of fulfillment . . ."

These points emerged more strongly in this part of the research than in the research literature. It appears that the lack of middle management structures in schools in Ireland and the lack of caretaking and support staff are seen to put an undeniable burden on principals to the point that women decide the job is not worth doing. Women will consider deeply before committing themselves to a job that is poorly supported.

Style of Management and its Impact

The importance of the role of the principal in leading the teaching staff and setting the tone of the school came across very clearly in the focus group discussions, and in particular the style of leadership used by the principal. It was suggested that the style of management in use in a school has an impact on the climate of the school and on the professional lives of teachers. A preference was expressed for a collaborative style that allowed for the empowerment of staff, as outlined in the literature review in Chapter 2. One participant commented on the change in her work with a change of principal, that she was now more involved in decision-making in the school. Speaking of the new principal she said:

> "She is very open to delegating a lot . . . she asks a lot more (than the previous principal) but you can suggest a lot more . . . that is very empowering and I find it tremendous to feel that the principal has confidence in your ability to represent the school."

An interviewee in a management position reported difficulties encountered in taking over as a woman with a different style of management to that of the previous incumbent. The experience as described reflected the research findings, as she found herself challenged by those who did not approve of her style and by those who saw the collaborative style of working with others as a sign of weakness (Shakeshaft, 1989).

POWER RELATIONS IN EDUCATION

Aspects of power relations are examined here in relation to the perceived attitudes of religious sisters in education, of other gatekeepers and of colleagues. The transfer from a religious principal to a lay principal introduces major changes to a school and gives an opportunity for staff to reflect more objectively on the management of the school. It also raises questions for teachers with regard to the possibility of a career as principal for themselves. In addition to the special circumstances that arise in Irish schools of a change over from religious to lay management, the question of the micro-politics of the staffroom arises. Ball (1987) identified the time period immediately after a new principal is appointed as a time when the micro-political situation in a school becomes more visible and the staff are very active politically, as members of staff attempt to retain or gain influence with the new principal.

Perceived Attitudes of the Gatekeepers

The religious sisters formed and still form an important group in education in that they played the role of principal and there was often another religious sister in the role of manager, in particular in single sex girls' primary and secondary schools. Thus they played a key role in an important section of schools in Ireland. While these roles have diminished, religious sisters and their male counterparts continue to play a role as gatekeepers for positions of principal in the schools controlled by the religious congregations and as trustees in community & comprehensive schools. They also hold the position of principal in a diminishing number of secondary and primary schools. The perceived attitudes of these religious are thus important in a number of ways. One participant in the focus group voiced the opinion that in her experience the religious sisters had fostered a particular type of teacher in their schools, namely an excellent classroom teacher, but one who did not get involved in policy decision-making and was happy to be passive and let the organisation be run "from above". She felt that such teachers were then not developed as "principal material" and that men or women from outside the school were being appointed as principals in such schools.

The issue of the attitudes and opinions of gate keepers and in particular the members of selection committees, with regard to the competence of women to manage and lead, is central to the appointment of principal, particularly as the male construct of management and leadership style is the commonly accepted one. Unless selection committees are aware of the impact of their attitudes and perceptions on their opinions of candidates and unless such attitudes are explicitly discussed, the dominant male construct may prevail.

In an equality case challenging an appointment for a temporary A post in 1985, the defense of the selection committee illustrates an instance in which different judgements were made of the candidates, a man and a woman. The selection committee stated with reference to the woman candidate:

> ... she was casual in her response to questions and assumed she could do the job since she was already familiar with some aspects of it (Equality Officer's Recommendation No. EE2/1985).

While for the successful candidate who was a man the selection committee stated that:

> He appeared positive and convincing regarding his ability to carry out the duties (required) . . . (Equality Officer's Recommendation No. EE2/1985).

The meaning of these two statements is an important issue here. One candidate who "assumed she could do the job" and another who "appeared convincing regarding his ability to carry out the duties" had a different impact on the selection committee. These statements are saying the same thing except that in one instance there is the pejorative use of the words "was casual" and in the other the candidate "appeared positive". This raises questions as to why it was that one could not convince the selection committee of her competence while the other could. The question here is how a selection committee judges a candidate and on what they are basing their judgements. Was this a failure on the part of the woman concerned or a failure of the selection committee to be gender fair, or was it an accurate judgement? It is not possible to decide from the "defence" of the selection committee, which by its language highlights the perceptions of the selection committee, as opposed to different qualities in the applicants.

Power Relations among Colleagues

The issue of power relations in the school emerged in the focus group discussion, particularly with regard to gender relationships in the staff room. One participant described the relationship between herself and some men on the staff in her school. She had applied for the principalship and had been called for a second interview, something which none of the male candidates from the staff had achieved. The appointment ultimately went to a man from outside the staff. This participant described receiving constant reminders of her failed application for the position and constant reminders of her age from some male colleagues. This is one example of "men behaving badly", identified by Coldron and Boulton (1998), termed "gender joking" by Cunnison (1989) which emerged during the discussions. Other examples included a woman who had a responsible position in education outside her school, where she was the only woman involved. Some of her male colleagues referred to her as the "token woman". While this term has a particular meaning in the literature (Chapter 2), this woman interpreted the term as meaning that she had not achieved the position in her own right, or because of her abilities but that she was in that position only because she was a woman. On the other hand, an individual interviewee related how she experienced more antagonism from women who resented her promotion than from men. This reflects the findings of Coldron and Boulton (1998). It would appear that the reaction of colleagues, both male and female, to a woman who is ambitious and/or capable can fall into the category of attempts at control by the use of power (Ball, 1987).

With regard to recent positive developments participants commented on the tendency for younger women to be ambitious and to seek further qualifications and promotion. A second major positive change identified by some included the changes in schools where posts of responsibility now involved teachers in much more challenging jobs and with much more authority. However, the overwhelming feeling, was that despite these positive changes, women are losing ground in management at a fast rate and that even though younger women are ambitious, they will not succeed in gaining ground in the system as it stands.

SUMMARY

The low rate of applications from women for principalships in secondary schools, which was noted in Chapter 4, was highlighted in the discussion with the focus group. This is a key issue in this study. While the focus group comprised women drawn exclusively from the secondary sector, many of the reasons which emerged in that discussion had already emerged in the literature: the pressure of caring work, the value that women place on family life, the lack of role models and peers in management, the problem of mobility, and the limited number of options open to women.

The four questions addressed in this chapter have illuminated the structures and processes in the educational system which influence the perceptions, attitudes and aspirations of women in relation to management in education.

There are perceived structural barriers in the system of promotions that discourage women from applying for principalships. Perceived structural barriers include: having to seek a recommendation from a person with power who disapproves of women in positions of authority; the lack of recognition of any but formal management experience; the gender imbalance of some interview boards and the confidential closed method in which criteria are agreed and candidates for principalships are selected.

Aspects of the Irish education system which appeared to discourage women from applying for promotion included a perception that an application for promotion would damage good working relationships with peers. Second, a perception by women that the role of principal required a commitment that they could not give because of the burden of caring work that they carried in the home, and that they valued their role in the home too much to endanger it. A further issue that may be of importance in the secondary sector is the lack of experience of carrying out responsible roles as part of a middle management team in a school.

Women's attitudes to career have been recognised as being based on the values held by women: the need to invest time in family relationships, the demands of caring work, the pressures women feel in relation to housework and the value they place on the quality of their life. Women's perception of the job of principal as demanding unreasonable amounts of time and the lack of support systems for principals are a major barrier to women's interest in promotion.

In discussion, aspects of power relations emerged which would discourage women from applying for promotion. If the question of application for promotion is perceived to give rise to difficulties in staff relations with peers or in veiled antagonism from other staff, and if the perceived attitudes of the gatekeepers are such that it is felt that it is pointless to apply, then application rates will be affected. Situations where gatekeepers do not see the importance of gender balance on a selection committee would be particularly discouraging.

While the filters identified in the first part of this chapter may create barriers to women's progress in promotion, each of these filters is controlled by the attitudes of the decision-makers to some degree. Thus attitudes are the key to change in the proportion of women in management in the future: the attitudes of women teachers themselves, the attitudes and behaviour of other teachers towards successful and unsuccessful candidates, the attitudes of the gatekeepers and the personnel involved in the support structures. The different approach to career of some women, compared with that of men, which informs their decisions in relation to career moves, means that the weaknesses in the present system of management will continue to cause women to decide that there are more important things in their lives than the management of a school in very difficult circumstances. If it is important that the "voice" of women is to be heard in education and the education system is to retain some balance in the management structures that are so important to schools, then these defects will need to be addressed.

Chapter 6

WOMEN INTO EDUCATIONAL MANAGEMENT: POSITIVE INTERVENTIONS

INTRODUCTION

One of the objectives of this research was to identify possible strategic interventions which could be developed to address the issues which have emerged and which would encourage women to play an increasing role in educational management. Critical issues identified in previous chapters include:

- The increasing feminisation of the profession in all sectors

- The evidence of inequalities in promotion to principalships in all age groups in the primary sector

- The decrease since 1986 in the proportion of women holding administrative principalships in the primary sector and an increase in those in teaching principal positions

- The continuing loss of women in principalships in the secondary sector and the very low rate of applications from women for that position within that sector

- The evidence of loss of promotion to women in the age groups over fifty, due in part to breaks in career, enforced or not, particularly in the community & comprehensive and vocational sectors

- The continuing differences in rates of promotion for younger women in the community & comprehensive and vocational sectors, related to low rates of applications for promotions within schools or sectors

- The variety of career blocks which limit the progress of women to the most powerful positions in organisations

- The fact that in primary and secondary schools, women have not been accustomed to compete for promotion, nor are they accustomed to leaving themselves open to comment and/or criticism from colleagues if they are unsuccessful in a bid for promotion

- The fact that women sometimes appear not to have thought through the implications of holding a senior position, perhaps in the belief that they would not be successful.

It is clear from the analysis in this study that unless some positive intervention strategies are put in place the gender imbalance in leadership positions will increase. The Education Commission of the Conference of Religious of Ireland (CORI) initiated such an intervention in 1993. This was as a result of a policy decision to address the under-representation of women in leadership positions in order to promote one of the goals of CORI:

> ... to actively promote justice for women in the Church and in civil society (Education Commission, CORI, p. ii).

The intervention took the form of organising and staging a seminar with a number of invited speakers from different perspectives in educational management. The Education Commission published the proceedings of the seminar along with a discussion paper entitled "Reflections and Recommendations of the Education Commission of the Conference of Religious of Ireland", which presented an analysis of issues related to the lack of women in educational management.

In their publication, the Education Commission of CORI set out an extensive positive action programme. One element of this programme was:

> The establishment of networks of support where existing holders of leadership posts take responsibility for identify-

ing and nurturing women who would subsequently become candidates for leadership positions (CORI, 1994, p. 59).

Recent research from Norway indicates that such a network system combined with in-service in education leadership has had a positive effect on the rate of applications from and appointments of women to management positions (Oftedal, 1997).

The Education Commission of CORI further proposed that a number of bodies such as the Department of Education and Science and the teacher unions should become involved in providing inservice in educational leadership for women. Gold (1996) also suggested that management development programmes could have a positive impact:

> If we are to have more women in educational management, they must be encouraged and they should have their professional skills and qualities recognised and reinforced. One of the most obvious ways for this validation to take place is on management development courses (Gold, 1996, p. 6).

A PILOT LEADERSHIP TRAINING PROGRAMME FOR WOMEN

In September 1997 the Equality Committee of the Department of Education and Science funded the development and delivery of a pilot training programme for women (Appendix 4). It was modelled on a leadership development programme which has run successfully in the Institute of Education in London University (Gold, 1993). This programme, called Women into Educational Management, was offered for a second time in February 1998. Twenty women from first and second-level schools participated in the initial three-day residential programme and 14 in the second.

When the first programme was advertised, over 60 requests for information were received and 21 applications were submitted before the deadline of 31 May 1997. Further requests for places or information continued to come in during the months following. Six of the participants were from primary schools, six from secondary schools, two from community schools and six from vocational schools. The range of teaching experience was from 12 years to 27 years and the level of management experience also varied. Two were principals of schools (primary), six were vice-principals and the rest were A or B post holders.

OBJECTIVES OF THE PROGRAMME

The pilot programme was designed specifically to address issues as outlined in the first part of this chapter and to initiate a process with a view to increasing the role of women in educational leadership. It was unique in terms of its context, the philosophy and methodology which underpinned it and in its presentation and organisation. The aim of the programme was to facilitate participants in their professional development by allowing time and space:

- For them to recognise their skills, knowledge and their potential contribution to educational management

- To empower them to develop a management vision and style true to their values and a clear vision of themselves as managers

- To develop an empowering open process which allows the sharing and development of skills, knowledge and strategies about management.

Murphy (1992) commented that the traditional hierarchical model of school management is no longer adequate and schools are being forced to shift from a hierarchical structure to one that promotes participation, communication, reflection and experimentation. As is evident in the literature (Chapter 2), women are more comfortable with this current approach to educational management. Fullan (1993) argues that the successful management of schools today demands leadership which is enabling, flexible and expert at dealing with change. Skills which are central to the successful management of schools include: the ability to work co-operatively with others, to promote dialogue, reflection, inquiry and an openness to change. Those involved in educational management need to develop and articulate their educational philosophy, values and vision. They need to have belief in their ability to lead others, the self-knowledge to recognise their own skills and the maturity to acknowledge the skills and wisdom of others. Thus, the focus of the programme was on the development of a personal management style with which the individual would feel comfortable. It proposed to initiate a process which would assist participants in clarifying their values in relation to education, and to model a style of co-operative working, communication and reflection which could be transferred to a leadership situation in schools.

PROGRAMME PHILOSOPHY AND METHODOLOGY

The philosophy/methodology underpinning this course was that of Kolb's cycle of experiential learning. This allows for critical reflection to follow action, then analysis leading to a further cycle of reflection and action, where the learner's professional experience is recognised and built on (Kolb, 1984). It can best be summarised as extracting principles from experience in order to plan strategies for the future. Commenting on Kolb's model, Gold (1996) states that:

> ... it offers the opportunity to find different ways of making sense of an experience, and acknowledges that there can be different solutions — there is no right or wrong solution, there are just solutions that fit certain situations more clearly, depending on values and circumstances (Gold, 1996, p. 9).

The pedagogical approach used in the programme allowed for the different stages of the cycle of learning to take place either on the course or in private at a later stage.

In recognition of the value of Kolb's (1984) cycle of learning, each session over the three days was designed to use a range of pedagogical approaches. In a short three-day program such as this, the "action" was replaced by group discussions or role-play. The programme included a wide variety of learning activities: icebreakers, small group discussions, large group discussions, working in pairs, brainstorming, role-play, case studies, hand-outs, individual private reflection time and use of a course diary. The importance of private reflection was particularly emphasised both in time allowed during the day and in individual evening work. Participants had an opportunity to internalise what was happening, to question and seek clarification and frame possible solutions at their ease. Answers did not have to be instantaneous and perfectly articulated.

The programme espoused the idea that adults learn best when they are involved, recognise that the programme meets a need, experience a variety of methods in a supportive environment and when they are enjoying themselves. The emphasis throughout was on interactive learning where the dominance of the teacher is reduced, the importance of the learner is increased and learners are afforded an opportunity to feel more effective. It was decided to avoid lengthy formal inputs with little time for discussion and reflection. The facilitators did not seek to be the providers of answers and solutions to a passive receptive audience. Instead, as indicated above, they sought to initiate and facilitate a *process* which invited participation, sharing, exploring and examining experiences, reflecting and planning. They saw themselves as participants with colleagues on a journey of self-discovery through reflection on experience and practice. Every effort was made to acknowledge and validate the professional experience of participants. Murphy (1992, p. 155) outlines a number of principles which he states should underpin management development programmes and which are in accordance with the approach outlined above. These include that:

- Learning should be student-centered
- Active learning should be stressed
- Personalised learning should be emphasised
- A balance of instructional approaches is needed
- Co-operative approaches to learning and teaching should be underscored.

For this methodology to work it had to take place within a particular *climate* of trust, openness, genuineness and mutual respect where participants felt comfortable in discussing their varied experiences. It was therefore essential to spend time at the outset developing an ethos to support this. In the early stages of the programme, a group contract was agreed in response to the question: "What qualities are important to ensure a good climate for learning during the coming days?" This was referred back to regularly, particularly at the beginning of each session, to ensure that everyone was still comfortable with what had been agreed and that it was being adhered to.

PROGRAMME CONTENT AND PRESENTATION

The range of topics covered in the three-day programme related to management and leadership in education. These included: vision and values, leadership styles, organisational dynamics, managing change, managing conflict and communications. While the topics in the timetable (Appendix 4) may appear to be similar to other management development courses, the thrust of this course was to raise issues, reflect on them and discuss them in the light of one's values and one's personal experience with a view to developing a personal management vision and style with which one could be comfortable. Participants were afforded an opportunity to reflect on educational management and why they should want to do it, to tap into qualities in themselves such as integrity, dedication, humility, openness and creativity and to experience and understand team work and collective responsibility.

Critical to the success of the programme were the empowering pedagogy and the presentation of the material. In espousing a management style that is democratic and participatory, emphasising collaborative community-building strategies, it was important for the facilitators to model this approach in their work. Therefore, the programme was co-facilitated, each facilitator playing to the partners' strengths and supporting the other as necessary. The collaborative approach to the design and delivery of each topic required intensive planning and co-operation and a sharing of tasks. It is important to point out that this approach and methodology made significant demands on the programme facilitators. While it is interesting and rewarding to work in this way, it demands an openness to questioning, a willingness to open up to other people and to be receptive to their experience and points of view. Essential ingredients for the success of this approach are good planning, a positive team spirit, a flexibility of approach and a willingness to review and adjust the programme as necessary.

PROGRAMME EVALUATION

The evaluation of the programme centred on an immediate and a long-term approach. At the end of each of the three-day sessions participants were requested to fill out an evaluation form (Appendix 5). Approximately six months afterwards a second questionnaire (Appendix 6) was issued to all participants. This postal evaluation related specifically to the long-term impact of the course and participants' personal plans for career changes.

In the initial evaluation the questions were open-ended, allowing for participants to make comments. Questions related specifically to the most helpful session, the least helpful session, the teaching methodology, suggestions for improvements, and invited comments on perceived barriers in putting the learning from the course into effect. Eighteen evaluation forms were returned at the end of the first course. From the second course, ten evaluation forms were returned.

The overall response to the programme was very positive. At the end of the first three-day session, 17 out of the 18 evaluations returned commented that the course was very effective (score of 1 on a scale of 1 to 5) and one found it effective (score of 2). Of the ten participants who responded at the end of the second course, nine found the course very effective and one found it effective. Both group sizes were appropriate for the type of methodology used — "the group gelled, shared and learned from each other" — and the mix of teachers from different sectors was enriching. The atmosphere was relaxed — "a relaxed and trusting atmosphere was created . . . there was a great sense of fun and enjoyment" — and the discussion was open and lively. General comments from participants included:

> "Best in-service course I have attended, ever . . ."
>
> "Very enjoyable and well presented . . ."
>
> "This was extremely worthwhile from all aspects — it will be remembered as a great experience . . ."
>
> "I really enjoyed the course very much . . ."
>
> "The course was excellent . . ."
>
> "It was a great opportunity and a wonderful experience . . ."

"Education in Ireland today needs courses like this..."

In response to a question on programme content and the topics considered most helpful, the session on conflict management was highlighted by the greater number of participants as being particularly relevant and helpful. More general comments in response to that question included, "All were absolutely wonderful" and "oh, everything". When commenting on the least helpful session, participants referred again to the session on conflict management commenting that more time could be given to it. The topic titled Management and Leadership had been covered by some participants in previous management courses so was repetitive for them. Another critical comment referred to the overload of programme content. It was felt that too much material was covered over the three days. This complaint was particularly evident in the evaluation at the end of the first course. Consequently, for the second course held in February 1998, the programme was amended allowing more time for in-depth work in certain areas and for reflection. Also some topics that participants had listed as suggested improvements were incorporated into the programme e.g., drawing up a *Curriculum Vitae*, interview techniques and questions.

With regard to the teaching methodology positive comments referred to the balance of input and discussions and the opportunity for individuals to contribute. Comments included:

> "It was easy to contribute in discussions: facilitation was very good..."

> "Short bursts of information followed by discussion was very helpful..."

> "Space and time for individuals to contribute was good."

One participant stated:

> "I didn't consider it was a teaching situation. I thought we were discussing issues..."

As stated earlier, emphasis was placed on the participation of the learners, thus ensuring "active learning" but also to ensure that the knowledge of participants was shared and valued. The following responses from participants suggest that this was successfully achieved:

> "Good participation . . ."
>
> "We were forced to act and think . . ."
>
> "I loved the stimuli, the active learning and the ensuing discussions . . ."
>
> "The variety in the workgroups helped promote interaction in the group. We learned from each other."
>
> "I felt valued for my contribution . . ."

Responses to the question regarding barriers to further career developments highlighted the success of the programme in facilitating the professional development of the participants. Comments from participants suggested that for the most part they had been refreshed, energised and empowered by the programme:

> "A great morale boost."
>
> "I feel more focussed . . ."
>
> "I return to my job rejuvenated, refreshed and enthusiastic . . ."
>
> "It just opened up an entire new world of hopes and possibilities. It refreshed me mentally. An exhilarating future . . ."
>
> "It gave me a helicopter view of my role in education . . ."
>
> "The course fulfilled my hopes, but surpassed my expectations."

In response to the specific question regarding perceived barriers in acting on the learning from the course, one participant commented:

> "I don't see any — I feel I have gained confidence and become more focused as to what my role in management is . . ."

Another stated:

> "Procrastination! There is no reason for not using this material to help me to develop and improve in my job."

However, some participants listed issues such as a lack of opportunities at primary level, the lack of a support network and lack of availability of information as barriers and two expressed an uncertainty of where they were going:

> "I feel I am personally at a crossroads . . ."

> "The barriers may only be my perception of where I am going".

Approximately six months after the completion of the second training programme a second questionnaire (Appendix 6) was issued to all 34 participants. This evaluation focussed specifically on the long-term impact of the course and participants' personal plans for career changes. Twenty-seven forms were returned (79 per cent).

The respondents reported a variety of changes in careers. Twelve had applied for promotion within their own school or elsewhere. Of these, seven were successful. One had been appointed acting deputy principal, one who was acting deputy principal was made permanent, two were appointed deputy principals, one was appointed to a post of responsibility, one was appointed a Department of Education and Science inspector and one a lecturer at third level. Of the 13 who responded reporting no change in career, two were already principals of schools. Two went on career break. With regard to career/study plans five stated that they intended to apply for further promotion but many left this section blank. Nine had embarked on further study.

With regard to the overall impact of the programme six participants reported that their confidence was increased by the course and a further six commented that they felt affirmed by what they had experienced. Comments included:

> "The course was energising and informative."
>
> "It was good for spurring people into action . . ."
>
> "It was enlightening and beneficial . . ."
>
> "Challenging and worthwhile."

Five had not intended applying for further promotion but changed their plans as a result of the course. Five mentioned the learning experience as very positive, referring to the hand-outs and bibliography as being useful. Other positive comments referred to the opportunity to reflect on personal issues and the opportunity to meet different people. One person stated that she would like to see a more active women's network in operation in education.

SUMMARY

It is evident from the above evaluation that this particular pilot programme was well received and successful in its aims. The methodology adopted worked well and the programme content met the needs of participants. In particular, the programme gave participants an opportunity to reflect on their potential contribution to educational management, it encouraged them to develop a vision of themselves as managers and facilitated their involvement in a process of dialogue, reflection and a sharing of skills and experience.

The responses in the evaluation forms indicate that participants benefited both personally and professionally from their involvement in the programme. They felt affirmed and energised and were happy to consider applying for promotional opportunities. It is encouraging to note that this "feel good" factor was still evident in the responses to the postal evaluation over a year after the delivery of the first programme.

As stated earlier, positive intervention strategies need to be put in place in order to redress the gender imbalance which currently exits in leadership positions in Irish education. This particular pilot programme offers a successful model for positive action in this regard.

Chapter 7

CONCLUSIONS AND RECOMMENDATIONS

INTRODUCTION

The objectives of this research focused on clarifying the position of women in education in Ireland with specific reference to the low proportion of women in educational management. The literature review informed decisions regarding the direction of the research.

An important focus of this study was necessarily the gathering of data which was hitherto not available but which was essential to the work. Data in all four sectors in education — primary, secondary, community & comprehensive and vocational — was gathered to enable a full analysis of the position of women in education and in educational management. As application rates for promotion by women appeared to be considerably lower than those of men, data was collected with regard to this issue. In the analysis of the findings, a number of questions arose that related to the experience, attitudes and perceptions of women and of those in decision-making positions in education, the gatekeepers. These were addressed using in-depth discussions with women teachers and others involved in educational management and policy formation. This chapter draws together the conclusions arising from the study and sets out recommendations for change.

CONCLUSIONS

The Feminisation Process

In Ireland, the feminisation of the teaching profession is evident across all sectors in education. While the current proportion of women in teaching is comparable with other European countries in both primary and second level, the situation in Ireland at second level is changing rapidly. Between 66 per cent and 75 per cent of recently appointed teachers in the second-level sectors are women. In the primary sector, the percentage of women is increasing but more slowly. While there is no data available on recent recruits, 84 per cent of younger teachers in the primary sector are women.

The rate of change in the gender balance of the teaching body varies between sectors. The primary and secondary sectors are continuing to become more feminised at a steady rate, as a higher proportion of new recruits are women compared with the number of women nearing retirement age. However, in the community & comprehensive and vocational sectors, the rate of feminisation will be greater because of the high proportion of male teachers over 50 combined with the high recruitment rate of women.

Women's and Men's Careers

In an analysis of the figures at primary level for a twenty-year period, 1976 to 1996, women show some loss in career time. All age groups have tended to remain in teaching, except those in the 20 to 29 age group (1986), who show a decrease in numbers of almost ten per cent over the following ten years. This may be as a result of women availing of career breaks.

In the secondary sector, considering the difficulty in obtaining permanent positions in the system in recent years, women start teaching relatively early. The evidence suggests that a proportion (around 12 or 14 per cent, over a ten-year period, 1985 to 1995) leave the profession in the childbearing years or perhaps move to a different sector in education or to a different career but that some return or begin teaching at a later age. However, in the two sectors examined, primary and secondary, there is a constant loss of men from either the profession or the sector. In the primary sector, the loss of men is consistently greater than the loss of women except for the age group 20-29 (1986). The loss of men is higher in the secondary sector, but this may represent movement to other sectors.

The information available on the community & comprehensive and vocational sectors did not allow an exploration of the above issue. However, there is evidence of a late start by men in the community & comprehensive sector but not in the vocational sector. In relation to loss of career time, both men and women show loss of career time in these sectors, although in the higher age groups, the losses for women are greater.

Gender and Promotion to Principalship

In the primary sector, more than 40 per cent of men are principals by the time they reach the age of 40, compared with ten per cent of women. By retirement age this progresses to a situation where more than 70 per cent of men are principals compared with just over 20 per cent of women. While the proportion of women in principalships is increasing, a number of key gender differences have emerged. First, women are more likely to lose their principalships when school amalgamations take place. Secondly, the participation patterns of women in the positions of teaching principal and administrative principal are different in that the number of women in administrative principalships dropped by a fifth in a ten-year period, 1986 to 1996. This pattern of women being appointed to principalships which involve teaching and which are in smaller schools is reflecting patterns discernible elsewhere in Europe (Chapter 2). No data is available on the level of applications from women for the different types of principalships and the success rate of women in these competitions.

In secondary schools the proportion of women principals has been declining as women religious leave these positions. Women have been appointed to the vacancies that arise in almost 30 per cent of these schools overall (ASTI, 1995). In coeducational schools across all three second-level sectors, the proportion of women appointed has been in the region of 20 per cent.

In the community & comprehensive sector, data on appointments to principalships relates to the period 1992 to 1994. In that period, women were appointed in 20 per cent of appointments to principalships (O'Hara, 1994). However, the proportion of women in principalships remains the lowest of any sector in 1996, at ten per cent.

In the vocational sector, there has been an increase in the proportion of principals who are women to just over 11 per cent. This represents an increase of over 100 per cent since 1985.

Other Promotional Posts

In primary and secondary schools, promotion has been based on seniority within the school up to the level of vice-principal. In both these sectors, women have been promoted to A and B posts and vice-principalships in comparatively large numbers to date. Discrepancies between the total proportion of women in the secondary sector and the proportion of women in vice-principalships posts may be due to loss of career time and therefore loss of seniority for women. The factors relating to the recent decline in the proportion of women vice-principals remain unknown.

In the sectors where appointments to all promotional posts have been on merit, the community & comprehensive and vocational sectors, women are poorly represented in all but the lowest promoted positions and the proportion of women decreases as the level of promotion rises. Inequalities are evident in the gender imbalance in senior posts (principal, vice-principal and A posts) in the community & comprehensive sector, with men twice as likely as women to be in these senior posts. While this imbalance is greatest in the age groups over 50, it is present to a degree in all age groups over 40. There are greater disparities in the vocational sector. Inequalities emerge in all age groups in this sector, with almost three-quarters of men promoted compared with less than half of women. In senior positions, the gender imbalance is more pronounced, with 15 per cent of women in senior positions compared with 40 per cent of men.

Applications for Promotion

While the proportion of women applying for principalships at primary level has increased consistently over a period of ten years, to reach over half of applicants in the period 1994 to 1996, this is still low considering the number of women in the teaching body.

In proportional terms men are three times more likely to apply for a principalship than women in this sector. The lack of data in relation to applications for different types of principalships leaves important questions, that need to be addressed, unanswered.

There is also a serious lack of data in the secondary sector in which the overall proportion of women applying for principalships appears to be the lowest of any sector. Again, this issue, which was beyond the scope of this research, needs to be addressed.

This study presents data collected for the first time in the area of applications not only for principalships and vice-principalships but also for A and B posts in the community & comprehensive and vocational sectors. However, recent data on appointments to principalships in community & comprehensive schools was not available at this time. While the general pattern is for women to be more willing to apply for the lower promotional positions, there are important differences in rates of application and success in these sectors.

Women account for just over 20 per cent of applications for positions of principal in the vocational sector in the period 1993-96, a figure which is comparable to the rate of applications from women for principalships in community & comprehensive schools in the period 1992-94 (17.7 per cent). The rate of applications from women for vice-principalships in the community & comprehensive sector has almost doubled since data was last collected in 1992-94, from over 20 per cent to just over 40 per cent in the period 1993 to 1996, but the success rate for these women was considerably below that of the men who applied. While the proportion of women applying for vice-principalships is not as high in the vocational sector, standing at just over 30 per cent, these women enjoyed a higher success rate than their counterparts in the community & comprehensive sector.

Women are shown to apply for A and B posts in community & comprehensive and vocational sectors in relatively large numbers. However, in the case of B posts in the vocational sector, they are not applying in the same proportions as men. As the duties associated with these posts are generally administrative duties that can be completed within the school day, this decision is unlikely to be related to the greater burden of caring work done by women.

The question then is what is happening in schools to discourage women from applying for these posts.

Women's Attitudes and Choices

There is evidence of inequalities in the outcomes regarding promotion in schools. Possible filters identified include: the belief of some women that they may have difficulty in getting a favourable reference, the decision about what type of application form to use, the decisions with regard to policies in short listing for interview and the decision regarding gender balance on interview boards. Some of these may indicate underlying attitudes relating to the nature of leadership in education or the "natural" abilities of women and men, which could lead to inadvertent discrimination against women or a "freezing out" of women from educational management. While the Department of Education and Science has issued new guidelines with regard to the gender balance of selection committees, the question remains as to whether this will be enforced, and by whom.

Other aspects of the process of promotion would need to be examined. Whatever the attitudes of gatekeepers, there is a perception that the perceived burden of caring work is a negative issue for women in interview situations. Indeed, there is evidence that it has been raised at times (Daly, 1989). It was also clear from discussions and from the research literature that many women tend to prefer a consultative, democratic style of management, both as their stated preference for their own style of management and also for how they prefer to *be* managed. Discussion of these issues is imperative in education circles. It remains a question as to how many selection committees discuss such issues in setting down criteria for the process of selection of a principal. The issue of the quality and gender fairness of the process of promotion needs to be addressed and a system set in place to ensure that all selection committees adhere to recognised systems of good practice.

The key issue identified in this research is the question of the low rate of applications from women for promotion at all levels. A number of issues relating to the particular circumstances of women in Irish schools emerged in discussions:

- The job of the principal as performed by some of the religious sisters was perceived as unrealistic for some women. In general, the demanding role of the principal and the lack of support structures and back-up may be discouraging factors for some women who value their family role and quality of life.

- Power relations and the micro-politics of staffrooms emerged as issues that can have negative consequences for women. It may be that women in secondary schools are not accustomed to a culture of competition and do not have to compete for promotion until the position of principal is available. There appears to be a reluctance to step out of the team of peers and put oneself forward for promotion because of the possible negative consequences for working relationships in the aftermath of the appointment, whether the woman is successful or not.

There is a personal cost in applying for a principalship, particularly if it is in one's locality or school, and most women who seek promotion do so in their own school. The cost may be in terms of damaged personal relations with colleagues, the fear of the type of "gender joking" reported in this study and elsewhere, or in terms of loss of self-esteem. If the perceived attitudes of the people with control in this area are negative, then it may be a rational choice for many women with ability and management potential not to apply for the position advertised.

A Positive Intervention

It is clear that unless positive strategies are put in place such as those outlined in Chapter 6, gender imbalance in leadership positions in the Irish education system will increase. Research in Norway indicates that a network system for women combined with in-service in education leadership had a positive effect on the rate of applications from women and their appointment to management positions (Oftedal, 1997). The Irish experience with regard to a pilot training programme as outlined in Chapter 6 was equally positive.

If women are to "step out of the shadows", and play a significant part in the management of schools and in the decision-making processes in education, then positive action must be taken.

RECOMMENDATIONS

Collection of Data and Research

This research has highlighted the lack of adequate data on the position of women in education in all sectors and in educational management in particular. The first set of recommendations, therefore, is in the area of record keeping. Action designed to affect gender imbalance cannot be evaluated unless there is a system in place to track changes in the gender balance in promotions in schools. It is essential that all promotional positions are centrally recorded and monitored.

It is recommended that:

- On an annual basis, the Department of Education and Science collect, analyse and publish records of applications and appointments to principalships by type of principalship, type of school and gender.

- Management bodies be given the necessary resources and be required to collect and publish records of applications and appointments by gender to all promotional posts which are filled by competition in the schools in their sector.

- Schools and vocational education committees be required to conduct an annual gender equality audit in relation to their employees. Such records could form part of a school plan and could be available for analysis on a national or regional level.

- Further research, quantitative and qualitative, be undertaken in a number of areas including power relations in schools, the values and attitudes of women in teaching, the reasons why women do not apply for promotional positions, the impact of feminisation and the late career start for men in some sectors of education.

Planning for Equality

In an effort to address the current gender imbalance it is essential that positive interventions in the form of in-service training are provided at different levels, with a view to effecting attitudinal change in a number of critical areas. It is recommended that:

- Training courses, in line with those outlined in Chapter 6, be made available to women in all sectors. These would have a number of aims: to encourage women to apply for leadership positions, to provide an opportunity for them to discuss their future options in a supportive environment, to provide a forum in which alternative styles of management can be discussed and analysed and to provide an opportunity for a system of support networks to be established. These courses could operate as part of inservice training provided and funded by the management bodies in the different sectors, or as an integral part of diploma courses in educational management or Masters in Education currently run by universities and Education Centres.

- The Department of Education and Science draw up guidelines on the composition and operation of selection committees and monitor same.

- Training courses be provided for prospective members of selection committees in schools. These courses would provide a forum in which alternative styles of management could be discussed and analysed, the issue of women in management be presented in a positive light and the effects of sex-role stereotyping on attitudes, assumptions and value judgements be highlighted. Again, these courses could be provided and funded by the management bodies in the different sectors or other competent authorities.

- The Department of Education and Science provide financial support to those organisations that initiate and implement positive intervention strategies.

- That issues such as gender balance in management and career development be incorporated into all pre-service teacher training.

Resources for Support Structures for Principals

It is recommended that:

- Proper ancillary services and secretarial staffing be provided at an appropriate level to schools in all sectors.

- Suitable support systems for teaching principals be established.

These recommendations, if put into effect, will not change the gender imbalance in educational management in the short term. However, in concert with a broad policy on gender equality in the education system, they would have a positive impact on the pressures leading to change. This research gives an indication of the direction such policy and action could take in order to ensure that women in Ireland play an increasing role in educational leadership in the new century.

Appendix 1

COLLECTION OF DATA

The data which is presented in this research, was requested from and supplied by the salaries sections (primary and second level) of the Department of Education and Science, Athlone, the Vocational Education Committees and individual community & comprehensive schools. The data supplied by the Department of Education and Science included a breakdown of the teaching body in secondary schools, by age, gender and the point on the salary scale for each teacher. In addition, information was supplied in relation to the promotional posts held by teachers in secondary schools and their age and gender. In relation to the primary sector the data supplied was age, gender and type of position held by teachers at three points in time, 1976, 1986 and 1996.

As each Vocational Education Committee keeps its own personnel records, data on permanent teachers which including details with regard to the age and sex of teachers on each point of the salary scale and details regarding promotional posts was requested from each Chief Executive Officer. Similar information was requested from the principals of community & comprehensive schools.

Additional information, relating to appointments to posts of responsibility and the rate of application for each post filled over a three-year period, was requested from all community & comprehensive schools and all Vocational Education Committees. In the case of community & comprehensive schools, the questions were confined to the positions of vice-principal, A posts and B posts.

Response

Not all Vocational Education Committees had complete records. One did not return any records. Two other Vocational Education Committees which are relatively large employers were unable to supply data on applications for posts of responsibility. Of the 77 community & comprehensive schools in existence at the time, 76 responded. In three cases, applications for posts of responsibility were affected by an internal agreement on seniority for promotion and these schools were excluded from the data on applications and appointments.

There were some key areas where it was not possible to gather data, in particular data in relation to applications for principalships in the secondary sector.

Appendix 2

DATA FOR TABLES 3.7A, 3.7B, 3.8A AND 3.8B

	Females, Secondary Schools								
	< 25	< 30	< 35	< 40	< 45	< 50	< 55	< 60	< 65
1									
2	0	0	0	0	0	1	1	0	0
3	133	89	28	15	4	1	1	0	0
4	107	108	26	7	8	5	1	3	0
5	63	192	47	12	7	5	3	1	0
6	14	216	66	19	10	10	3	1	1
7	1	208	84	29	16	4	5	4	0
8	0	143	119	27	17	6	5	1	1
9	0	85	160	30	23	11	3	3	0
10	0	34	152	38	8	9	7	1	0
11	0	6	142	50	11	11	7	1	0
12	0	0	162	63	10	11	8	1	1
13	0	0	122	81	8	13	8	2	1
14	0	0	57	74	16	12	5	7	1
15	0	0	0	167	33	16	6	7	2
16	0	0	11	154	39	15	9	3	3
17	0	0	16	99	21	11	5	4	2
18	0	0	0	27	176	36	14	13	3
19	0	0	0	114	120	37	9	9	5
20	0	0	0	139	77	17	14	7	2
21	0	0	0	162	56	26	6	1	1
22	0	0	0	1	104	110	18	10	5
23	0	0	0	0	169	58	32	13	6
24	0	0	0	0	155	47	17	11	7
25	0	0	0	2	218	49	19	9	5
26	0	0	0	0	28	493	395	286	145
Total	318	1081	1192	1310	1334	1014	601	398	191

	Indicates more advanced than expected		Indicates on expected point		Indicates delay in career

Appendix 3

QUALITATIVE METHODS

The issues that emerged in the research literature in Chapter 2 and in the data presented in Chapters 3 and 4 raised questions about the perceptions and attitudes of women teachers. While an exploration of these issues could form a study in itself, it was considered important in the context of this study to analyse some of the processes involved in producing the situation presented.

A qualitative approach was adopted as these methods are particularly oriented towards exploration and discovery (Patton, 1987) and are most appropriate for in-depth inquiries (Zyzanski *et al*, 1992). A number of methods were used. A day-long focus group discussion with women from secondary schools yielded considerable data. Details of the composition of the focus group are given below. Women teachers from secondary schools with a lay principal were invited to attend. It was considered that these teachers would likely have experienced the appointment of a lay principal and possibly have been aware of the exposure of the micro-politics that frequently occurs when a new principal takes up the position (Ball, 1987). A second source of data was a series of semi-structured interviews with individuals involved in policy formation, management or teaching in the primary, secondary, community & comprehensive and vocational sectors. A semi-structured rather than the structured interview was chosen as it allows the interviewee to talk about what is of significance to him/her, but within a predetermined framework of issues which the interviewer considered important. According to Borg and Gall (1989) the semi-structured interview provides a desirable combination of objectivity and depth and often provides valuable data that could not be obtained by any other means.

The Focus Group

Forty secondary schools with lay principals were circulated and principals were asked to inform women teachers of the planned seminar. The letter stated that the seminar was for women with administrative experience in education. Thirteen women from 11 schools in counties Dublin, Kildare and Louth were subsequently invited to attend the seminar.

No teachers from co-educational schools were involved in the focus group discussion. Four teachers were from single sex boys' schools, of which two were fee-paying. The remainder (nine teachers from seven schools) were from single-sex girls' schools, one of which was fee paying. In each of the single sex boys' schools the principal was a man, while in the single sex girls' schools, there were three men and four women principals.

Only one of the teachers who attended did not hold a post of responsibility. She had administrative experience as Transition Year Co-ordinator. Nine of the remaining teachers held A posts and three held B posts. The day was organised as a seminar in which discussion was guided by a facilitator. The agenda included broad areas such as recent change in education and the barriers to women's career development.

Appendix 4

WOMEN INTO EDUCATIONAL MANAGEMENT: PROGRAMME

Day 1 Thursday 25th September

15.30   Registration and light refreshments
16.00   Visions and values in educational management
18.00   The context for women
20.00   Dinner

Day 2 Friday 26th September

09.30   Management and leadership
13.00   Lunch
14.30   The micro-politics of schools
16.30   The management of change
17.50   Break
19.00   Meeting with guests, followed by dinner

Day 3 Saturday 27th September

09.30   Managing conflict
12.30   Lunch
13.30   Communications
14.30   Action plans and evaluation.
16.00   Light refreshments and closure.

Appendix 5

EVALUATION FORM

Participants were requested to fill in the following form with considerably more space for answers.

Women into Educational Management Programme Evaluation Form

Date:

1. How would you rate this course in general? Please ring the appropriate number below:

Very effective		Effective		Ineffective
1	2	3	4	5

2. Which parts of the programme were the most helpful/useful to you?

3. Which parts of the programme were the least helpful to you? Why?

4. Have the teaching methods used been:
    Helpful to your learning?
    Unhelpful to your learning?
    In what way?

5. Bearing in mind the time limitations, is there anything you would wish to have included which would improve the course?

6. What are likely to be the greatest barriers preventing you from using the learning on this course in your work?

7. Any other comments?

8. Are you a teacher at
    Primary   ☐
    Second level   ☐
        Which sector:
        Vocational   ☐
        Voluntary Secondary   ☐
        Community/Comprehensive   ☐

Appendix 6

EVALUATION FORM 2

Please fill in the following questionnaire and return to Leonie Warren

A reflection on the Women into Educational Management Course and on its impact or lack of impact on your life and career:

1. Has your position or role changed in your school? If so, in what way and why?

2. Have you applied for any promotional positions

In your own school?	☐
In another school?	☐
In another institution?	☐

Were you successful or not?

Will you apply again? Why/Why not?

3. Have you changed your career plans in the past year? If so, in what way and why?

4. Any other comments on the impact of the course?

Thank you for your co-operation.

BIBLIOGRAPHY

Acker, S. (1983) "Women and Teaching: A Semi-detached Sociology of a Semi-profession", in Walker, S. and Barton, L. (eds.), *Gender, Class and Education*, London: Falmer Press.

Acker, S. (1994) *Gendered Education*, Buckingham: Open University Press.

Adler, S., Laney, J. and Packer, M. (1993) *Managing Women*, Buckingham: Open University Press.

Adkison, J. (1981) "Women in School Administration: A Review of the Research", *Review of Educational Research*, 51 (3) pp. 311-343.

Al-Khalifa E. (1989) "Management by Halves: Women Teachers and School Management", in De Lyon, H. and Widdowson Magniuolo F., (eds.), *Women Teachers: Issues and Experiences*, Milton Keynes: Open University Press.

Alimo-Metcalfe, B. (1995) "An Investigation of Female and Male Constructs of Leadership and Empowerment", *Women in Management Review*, 10 (2) pp. 3-8.

Association of Secondary Teachers of Ireland, (1990) *The Promotional Expectations and Achievements of Teachers*, Dublin: ASTI.

Association of Secondary Teachers of Ireland, (1988-1997) *ASTI Convention Reports*, Dublin: ASTI.

Ball, S.J. (1987) *The Micro-Politics of the School: Towards a Theory of School Organisation*, London: Methuen & Co. Ltd. Reprinted by Routledge in 1993.

Blackmore, J. (1993) " 'In the Shadow of Men': The Historical Construction of Administration as a Masculinist Enterprise", in Blackmore, J. and Kenway, J., (eds.), *Gender Matters in Educational Administration and Policy*, London: The Falmer Press.

Blackwell, J. (1986) *Women in the Labour Force*, Dublin: Employment Equality Agency.

Borg, W.R. and Gall, M.D. (1989) *Educational Research: An Introduction*, White Plains: Longman.

Boulton, P. and Coldron, J. (1998) "Why Women Teachers Say 'Stuff It' to Promotion: a Failure of Equal Opportunities?", *Gender and Education*, 10 (2), pp. 149-161.

Buchan, L. (1980) "It's a Good Job for a Girl (But an Awful Career for a Woman!)", in Spender, D. and Sarah, E. (eds.), *Learning to Lose*, London: The Women's Press.

Campani, G. and Picciolini, A. (1997) "Italy", in Wilson, M. (ed.), *Women in Educational Management: A European Perspective*, London: Paul Chapman Publishing Ltd.

Case, S. (1994) "Gender Differences in Communication and Behaviour in Organisations", in Davidson, M.J., and Burke R.J. (eds.), *Women in Management: Current Research Issues*, London: Paul Chapman Publishing Ltd.

Cockburn, C. (1991) *In the Way of Women: Men's Resistance to Sex Equality in Organisations*, London: The Macmillan Press Ltd.

Coldron, J. and Boulton, P. (1998) "The Success and Failure of Positive Action to Mitigate the Effects of an All-male Senior Management Team in a Secondary School", *British Educational Research Journal*, 24, (3), pp. 317-331.

Cunnison, S. (1989) "Gender Joking in the Staffroom", in Acker, S. (ed.), *Teachers, Gender and Careers*, Lewes: Falmer Press.

Daly, M. (1989) "The Under-Representation of Female Post Primary Teachers in Promotional Posts", unpublished M.Ed. Thesis, University College Dublin.

Diamond, E. (1987) "Theories of Career Development and the Reality of Women at Work", in Gutek, B. and Larwood, L. (eds.), *Women's Career Development*, California: Sage Publications.

Drudy, S. and Lynch, K. (1993) *Schools and Society in Ireland*, Dublin: Gill and Macmillan.

Dunlap, D. M. (1995) "Women Leading: An Agenda for A New Century", in Dunlap, D. M. and Schmuck, P. A. (Eds.), *Women Leading in Education*, Albany New York: State University of New York Press.

Dweck, C. (1975) "The Role of Expectations and Attributions in the Alleviation of Learned Helplessness", *Journal of Personality and Social Psychology*, 31 (4) pp. 674-685.

Education Commission of the Conference of Religious of Ireland (1993) "Preface", *Women for Leadership in Education*, Dublin: Conference of Religious of Ireland.

Education Commission of the Conference of Religious of Ireland (1993) "Reflections and Recommendations of the Education Commission of the Conference of Religious of Ireland", *Women for Leadership in Education*, Dublin: Conference of Religious of Ireland.

Eisenstein, H. (1993) "A Telling Tale from the Field", in Blackmore, J. and Kenway, J., (eds.), *Gender Matters in Educational Administration and Policy*, London: The Falmer Press.

Evetts, J. (1989) "Married Women and Career: Career History Accounts of Primary Headteachers", *Qualitative Studies in Education*, 2 (2) pp. 89-105.

Evetts, J. (1990) *Women in Primary Teaching: Career Contexts and Strategies*, London: Unwin Hyman.

Evetts, J. (1994) *Becoming a Secondary Headteacher*, London: Cassell.

Fave-Bonnet, M. (1997) "France", in Wilson, M. (ed.), *Women in Educational Management: A European Perspective,* London: Paul Chapman Publishing Ltd.

Fullan, M. (1991) *The New Meaning of Educational Change*, London: Cassell.

Fullan, M. (1993) *Change Forces: Probing the Depths of Educational Reform*, Philadelphia PA: Falmer Press.

Gibbons, D. (1996) "Male Ethos and Male Management Culture in Some Public Sector Schools: An Analysis of Issues in the Irish Context", unpublished M.Eq. St. Thesis, University College, Dublin.

Gold, A. (1993) "'Women-friendly' Mmanagement Development Programmes", in Ouston, J. (ed.), *Women in Education Management*, England: Longman Group.

Gold, A. (1994) "Women into Educational Management", in Olroyd, D. and van Wieringen, F. (eds.) *European Issues in Educational Management*, De Lier: Academisch Boeken Centrum.

Gold, A. (1996) "Women into Educational Management", Paper presented to the European Union Conference: Gender Equality for 2 000 and Beyond, Dublin: Department of Education.

Gold, A. and Evans, J. (1998) *Reflecting on School Management*, London: Falmer Press.

Government of Ireland (1998) *Education Act*, Dublin: Government Publications Office.

Grant, R. (1987) "A Career in Teaching: A Survey of Middle School Teachers' Perceptions with Particular Reference to the Career of Women Teachers", *British Educational Research Journal*, 13 (3) pp. 227-239.

Grant, R. (1989) "Women Teachers' Career Pathways: Towards an Alternative Model", in Acker, S. (ed.), *Teachers, Gender and Career*, London: Falmer Press.

Gray, H.L. (1987) "Gender Considerations in School Management", *School Organisation*, 17 (3) pp. 297-302.

Gross N. and Trask A. (1976) *The Sex Factor and the Management of Schools*, New York: John Wiley.

Gutek, B. and Larwood, L. (1987) *Women's Career Development*, California: Sage Publications.

Hall, V. (1993) "Women in Educational Management: A Review of the Research in Britain." in Ouston, J. (ed.), *Women in Education Management*, England: Longman Group.

Hall, V. (1996) *Dancing on the Ceiling: A Study of Women Managers in Education*, London: Paul Chapman Publishing Ltd.

Hannan, D. F., Smyth, E., McCullagh, J., O'Leary, R., McMahon, D. (1996) *Coeducation and Gender Equality: exam performance, stress and personal development*, Dublin: Oak Tree Press.

Hill, M. and Ragland J. (1995) *Women as Educational Leaders: Opening Windows, Pushing Ceilings*, California: Corwin Press.

Hilsum, S. and Start, K. B. (1974) *Promotions and Careers in Teaching*, Slough: National Foundation for Educational Research.

Irish National Teachers' Organisation (1987-95) Reports to the Central Executive Committee, Equality Section, Dublin: INTO.

Irish National Teachers' Organisation (1995) *Male/Female Imbalance in Primary Education*, Dublin: INTO.

Kanter, R. M. (1977) *Men and Women of the Corporation*, New York: Basic Books.

Kanter, R. M. (1991) "Change-Master Skills: What it takes to be creative", In Henry, J., and Walker, D. (eds.) *Managing Innovation*, London: Sage.

Kellaghan T. and Fontes, P. (1985) *Gender Inequalities in Primary School Teaching*, Dublin: Educational Company.

Kolb, D. A. (1984) *Experiential Learning*, New Jersey: Prentice-Hall.

Kontogiannopoulou-Polydorides, G. and Zambeta, E. (1997) "Greece" in Wilson, M. (ed.), *Women in Educational Management: A European Perspective*, London: Paul Chapman Publishing Ltd.

Lacey, C. (1977) *The Socialisation of Teachers*, London: Methuen.

Larwood, and Gutek (1987), "Working Towards a Theory of Women's Career Development, in Gutek, B. and Larwood, L. (Eds.), *Women's Career Development,* California: Sage Publications.

Laemers, M. and Ruijs, A. (1996) "Statistical Portrait", *Context,* 12, pp. 7-15.

Leggatt, T. (1970) "Teaching as a Profession", in Jackson, J. A. (Ed.), *Professors and Professionalism*, Cambridge: Cambridge University Press.

Lortie D. C. (1975) *Schoolteacher: A Sociological Study*, Chicago Il: University of Chicago Press.

Lynch, K. (1994) "Women Teach and Men Manage", in *Women for Leadership in Education*, Dublin: Conference of Religious of Ireland.

Lynch, K. (1997) "Ireland" in Wilson, M. (ed.), *Women in Educational Management: A European Perspective*, London: Paul Chapman Publishing Ltd.

Lynch, K. (1999) *Equality in Education*, Dublin: Gill and Macmillan.

Marshall, J. (1984) *Women Managers: Travellers in a Male World*, Chichester: Wiley.

Moran, P. (1993) "Teacher Experience: Gender and Career", unpublished M.Ed. Thesis, University College, Dublin.

Mullarkey, M. (1994) "Women in Educational Leadership: Secular Female Principals in Irish Post-Primary Schools", unpublished M.Ed. Thesis, University College, Galway.

Murphy, J. (1992) *The Landscape of Leadership Preparation, Reframing the Education of School Administrators*, California: Corwin Press.

O'Connor, P. (1998) *Emerging Voices: Women in Contemporary Irish Society*, Dublin: Institute of Public Administration.

Oftedal, J. (1997) "Norway", in Wilson, M. (Ed.), *Women in Educational Management: A European Perspective*, London: Paul Chapman Publishing Ltd.

O'Hara, M. B. (1994) "Women as Principals: A Study in Community and Comprehensive Schools", unpublished M.Sc. in Ed. Man. Thesis, University of Dublin.

Ouston, J. (1993) "Women as Managers" in Ouston, J. (ed.), *Women in Education Management*, England: Longman Group.

Ozga, J. (1993) *Women in Educational Management*, Buckingham: Open University Press.

Patton, M.Q. (1987) *How to Use Qualitative Methods in Evaluation*, London: Sage.

Ruane, F. P. and Sutherland, J. M. (1999) *Women in the Labour Force*, Dublin: Employment Equality Agency.

Schmuck, A. and Dunlap, D. M. (1995) "Introduction", in Dunlap, D. M. and Schmuck, A. (Eds.), *Women Leading in Education*, Albany, New York: State University of New York Press.

Shakeshaft, C. (1989) *Women in Educational Administration*, California: Sage Publications.

Shakeshaft, C. (1993) "Women in Educational Management in the United States", in Ouston, J. (Ed.), *Women in Education Management*, England: Longman Group.

Valdez, R. and Gutek, B. (1987) "Family Roles: A Help or a Hindrance For Working Women", in Gutek, B. and Larwood, L. (Eds.), *Women's Career Development*, California: Sage Publications.

Vermeulen, A. and Ruijs, A. (1997) "The Netherlands", in Wilson, M. (Ed.), *Women in Educational Management: A European Perspective*, London: Paul Chapman Publishing Ltd.

Warren, L. (1996) "Women in Educational Management: Ireland", Paper presented to the European Union Conference: Gender Equality for 2 000 and Beyond, Dublin: Department of Education.

Warren, L. (1997) "The Career Structure of Women in Education", *Irish Educational Studies*, 16, pp. 69-84.

Weiner, G. (1994) *Feminisms in Education: an introduction*, Buckingham: Open University Press.

White, B. (1995) "The Career Developments of Successful Women", *Women in Management Review*, 10 (3) pp. 4-15.

Wilson, M. (1997a) "England and Wales", in Wilson, M. (Ed.), *Women in Educational Management: A European Perspective*, London: Paul Chapman Publishing Ltd.

Wilson, M. (1997b) "Overview", in Wilson, M. (Ed.), *Women in Educational Management: A European Perspective*, London: Paul Chapman Publishing Ltd.

Wilson, V. (1997) "Focus Groups: a useful qualitative method for educational research?", *British Educational Research Journal*, 23, (2), pp. 209-224.

Zanna, M., Crosby, F. and Loewenstein, G. (1987) "Male Reference Groups and Discontent Among Female Professionals", in Gutek, B. and Larwood, L. (eds.), *Women's Career Development,* California: Sage.

Zyzanski, S., McWhinney, I., Blake, R., Crabtree, B. and Miller, W. (1992) "Qualitative Research: Perspectives on the Future", in Crabtree, B.F. and Miller, W.L. (eds.), *Doing Qualitative Research*, London: Sage.